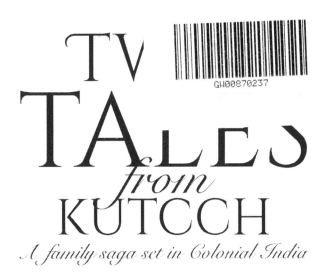

TALES from KUTCCH

A family saga set in Colonial India

SAEED IBRAHIM

INDIA · SINGAPORE · MALAYSIA

Notion Press

Old No. 38, New No. 6
McNichols Road, Chetpet
Chennai - 600 031

First Published by Notion Press 2019
Copyright © Saeed Ibrahim 2019
All Rights Reserved.

ISBN 978-1-68466-820-5

In Loving Memory of my parents

Contents

Author's Note

This book is a period fiction set in colonial India. Certain historical facts, events and personalities have been used to serve as a suitable backdrop to the prevailing times and to provide a historical perspective to the narrative. Apart from the ten main protagonists from the two families highlighted in the story, all other names, characters, places and incidents are either the product of the author's imagination or are used fictitiously and any resemblance to any actual person, living or dead, events or locales is entirely coincidental.

Preface

It is fascinating how heirlooms and cherished family possessions carry a story behind them revealing details not only about the object itself and its original owner or owners, but also about the social atmosphere and the cultural ethos of the times in which they lived. These narratives and family histories offer an invaluable means of preserving culture and customs, legacies and traditions, and in the process not only add to our knowledge but also provide a certain nostalgic appreciation of our past.

My inspiration for writing this book was derived from two heirlooms that had come down in my family from the colonial era of the late 19th century. The first was a bone china tea service which was from my great grandfather on my paternal side and the second was a framed citation or *sanad* presented to my great grandfather on my maternal side. The more I contemplated these two relics from my family's past, the more determined I was to find out details about their origins and more importantly details about my two 19th century great grandparents from whom we had inherited these items.

As my research into the lives and times of my two Kutcchi ancestors progressed, I was prompted to delve deeper. Armed with a clearer and more informed understanding of the background and events of the age in which they lived, the characters from the past seemed to come alive and I became convinced more than ever that I had to tell their story, albeit in a fictionalized setting.

The two central historically documented events that were crucial to the narrative were the maritime tragedy of 8th November 1888 which came to be known in later years as the "Titanic of Gujarat," although in actual fact the RMS Titanic sank 24 years later in April 1912. The SS Vaitarna (nick named "Vijli" or electricity) on her maiden voyage from Bhuj to Bombay, sank and disappeared mysteriously off the coast of Gujarat. My great grandparents who lived in Bhuj (the capital of the erstwhile semi-autonomous princely state of Kutcch in Gujarat) were travelling on the ship and they both met a tragic end when their ship was wrecked after a violent cyclonic storm, leaving no survivors.

My great grandfather on my maternal side, who lived in Malegaum (known today as Malegaon) was honoured with the title of Khan Sahib on 21st May 1898 by the then Viceroy of India, Lord Elgin for his services and contribution for the upliftment of the migrant weaving community of Malegaum. But regrettably he and his wife also met with an untimely death, again in an unforeseen accident.

The great grandparents on both sides, who at the time were unknown to each other, left behind young orphaned daughters to be brought up in Bombay by their respective aunts. This is the poignant story of these two remarkable women as they grapple with their loss, growing from childhood to womanhood, marriage and motherhood - a compelling narrative offering a fine blend of nostalgia, historical detail, tradition and family lore and at the same time touching on subjects such as the status of women, communal co-existence and the plurality of religious traditions and cultures, issues so relevant even today.

– Saeed Ibrahim
Bangalore, December 2018

PART 1

BHUJ – 1888-1895

Victoria Terminus – Completed 1888

Prag Mahal Palace, Bhuj

Blue & Gold Bone China Tea Service

The Absent Daughter

Jan Mohammed sat in his favourite easy chair on the wide verandah of his comfortable four room bungalow with a copy of the Gujarati newspaper the *Bombay Samachar* spread out in front of him. Although since 1855 the newspaper had graduated from a bi-weekly to a daily, it took days before his copy reached him in Bhuj. By then the news was already a bit out-dated, but Jan Mohammed eagerly awaited the delivery of his newspaper as it helped him keep abreast of events in Bombay (now known as Mumbai) and the happenings in the business community there. This day in May 1888 he read about the completion of Bombay's Victoria Terminus, that architectural marvel in the Indo-Saracenic style designed by the British architect Frederick William Stevens to commemorate the Golden Jubilee of Queen Victoria who had completed fifty years as a monarch. He remembered how the work on the new railway station had started a decade earlier in 1878 on the site of the old Bori Bunder station from where on the 16th April 1853, the Great Indian Peninsula Railway had operated the first passenger train from Bori Bunder to

Thana covering a distance of 39 km and heralding the birth of the Indian Railways.

But now his musings about the new Victoria Terminus were interrupted by the arrival of Imtiaz, the local barber who came to the house twice a week to give Jan Mohammed his customary shave and beard trim. After meticulously finishing the task at hand, Imtiaz ingratiatingly held up a hand mirror before his client's face to seek his approval. Jan Mohammed looked up to see his image reflected in the mirror. At 48, his face with its wide set eyes, straight nose and broad forehead was still handsome and unlined, although the hair on his head and his beard had a generous sprinkling of grey, which, according to some, gave him a more dignified appearance.

To Imtiaz he gave a curt nod of his head to indicate his satisfaction. It always helped to keep Imtiaz in check because he was the town's gossip monger and loved chatting up his clients in between cutting their hair or shaving their beards. But at Jan Mohammed's house he knew better and always remained uncharacteristically tight lipped. Jan Mohammed reached into his pocket and paid Imtiaz his dues and thought reminiscently of the story his father would tell the children to illustrate how barbers had always been known for their indiscretion and their inability to keep a secret.

His father, who always loved an audience, would clear his throat and start:

"In the old days, the town barber would not be paid for his services in cash, but rather in kind– a bag of grain or a *seer* of oil and often, if there was a marriage in the family, a brand-new item of clothing, invariably, a *sherwani.*

Thus, the barber's wardrobe was always well stocked and he was never short of clothes. Now it so happened, (his father would continue), that a friend of the barber's was getting married but did not have a *sherwani* to wear for the occasion.

'Why do you worry my friend, I have a yet unused *sherwani* at home and I would be happy to loan it to you and get you out of your predicament,' the barber offered. The groom was overjoyed and gladly accepted the generosity of his friend. Now as they stood outside to welcome the guests, both attired in shining new *sherwanis*, the barber piped up: 'Welcome, welcome, do come in. But make no mistake. My friend here is the groom, but the *sherwani* is mine.' The groom went scarlet with embarrassment and quietly whispered to the barber, 'Why did you have to say anything about the *sherwani*?' 'I am sorry', countered the barber, 'I will not say anything next time.'

But unable to keep the matter under his hat, when the next lot of guests passed by, he exclaimed, 'This here is the groom, and the *sherwani* is also his.' The groom now was beginning to get angry at his friend's indiscretion and remonstrated again with him. His friend with profuse apologies promised that he would no longer say anything. However, unable to contain himself, as the last lot of guests trooped in, he blurted out, 'Here is the groom, and of course there can be no mention of the *sherwani*,'" Jan Mohammed's father would end dramatically amidst peals of laughter.

Smiling to himself at the memory of this amusing story, Jan Mohammed stepped into the house to check with his wife Hajra if she had kept his bath water ready. Knowing that her husband liked his bath water plentiful and hot, Hajra had earlier made sure that Sakina, her house help had topped up the water and installed hot burning coals in the large bronze *samovar* in the bathroom.

Sakina was from the nearby village of Dahisara. Her husband had left her for another woman with two little girls to bring up. She had moved to Bhuj fifteen years ago in search of employment. It had been a difficult time with two small mouths to feed, but she was a proud and courageous woman. She had found cleaning and cooking work in five different households at each of which she toiled for two hours every day. It was back breaking work, but over the years she had managed to bring up and marry off her two daughters. Now, aged fifty years she felt it was time she settled down to full time work in a single household. Hajra herself had been looking for live-in house help and she readily employed Sakina. It had now been two years since Sakina had come to work for her and Hajra had been impressed by her sincerity, hard work and cheerful nature and the two women got along well together.

Jan Mohammed stepped out of his bath and began getting dressed, putting on a pair of starched white *pyjamas* tapered at the ankles and a long knee-length white *kurta* topped by a short, buttoned-up waistcoat. Summers in Bhuj were extremely hot and he wore his *sherwani* and red tasselled fez cap only for more formal occasions.

"Breakfast is ready *Sait*", Hajra called out in Kutcchi, the language they spoke between themselves. It was not the custom for good Kutcchi wives to address their husbands by their first names and Hajra used the more respectful "*Sait*" whilst addressing her husband. They both were also conversant in Gujarati and Urdu, and Jan Mohammed in English as well, although Gujarati was the language in which all local business was conducted. The couple now sat down to a breakfast of *sevian* topped with sugar, warm milk and thick fresh cream and crisp, deep fried *pakwan*, enjoyed plain or dunked into hot cardamom - flavoured tea.

But the house seemed somehow empty without Aisha, their demure and mild-mannered sixteen-year-old daughter. Aisha's clear and unblemished olive skin and large brown eyes made her a pretty and poised young lady, but unlike her mother's exuberance and robust good health, she had a more delicate physique and a shy, retiring nature.

Hajra's older sister Halima was married to Rehman, Jan Mohammed's cousin and they had settled in Bombay. They had two daughters only a few years older than Aisha and on their last trip to Bombay Hajra had been persuaded by her sister to allow Aisha to stay back. Being an only child, she was often lonely back home in Bhuj and the company of her cousins and the boisterous air of Halima's household in Bombay would do her good according to her aunt. Besides, she reasoned, Jan Mohammed could easily take her back on his next trip to Bombay which he made at least twice a year combining both business and a family visit.

Hajra had appeared convinced and had agreed to the proposal, but now barely a month down the line she was already missing her daughter and had begun to have second thoughts about her decision to leave her back in Bombay. Little did Hajra know at the time, how inexorably her decision was to affect the future course of events in their lives.

Business as Usual

As with the other Kutcchi Memon families living in Bhuj, Jan Mohammed and Hajra were descended from the Lohana Memon families living in Thatta in Sindh who had converted to Islam in the 15th century A.D. and subsequently left Thatta and migrated to Gujarat. They had come to be known as "*Momins*" or believers. The word "*Momin*" was corrupted later on to "Memon". Some families travelled to Bhuj and decided to settle down there. This group of Memons came to be known as Kutcchi Memons. From 1813 or 1816 onwards some Kutcchi Memons started moving out of Bhuj, seeking their fortune in other cities in India and overseas, but notably Bombay, attracted by its business opportunities.

From his Kutcchi Memon ancestry, Jan Mohammed had inherited a strong business acumen coupled with qualities of honesty, integrity and generosity, qualities that had gained for him the respect and goodwill of other members of Bhuj society, and in particular the trust and affection of his Parsee business partner, Jamshedji Khersetji Madon. Together they had set up "Jan & Co." a thriving silver ware and crockery outlet located in the Camp area of Bhuj.

The Camp area of Bhuj was an area located beyond the old walled city and at the foot of the Bhujia Hill. This was the area where in 1819, the British forces had set up "camp" after capturing the hill fort of Bhujia and establishing their authority over the area, which until then had been part of the independent princely state of Kutcch. The area had since become known as the Camp area and by the latter part of the 19th century, the Camp area of Bhuj had become a prosperous and almost exclusive quarter inhabited by the British officers and their households and some of the more affluent and influential Indian families.

It was just before 10 o'clock each morning that Jan Mohammed set out in his horse-drawn buggy to join his partner at the shop. Hajra on the other hand, having seen off her husband, would continue with the rest of her morning routine, supervising Sakina as she got her to dust and clean the house and wash the clothes and help Hajra in the kitchen with the preparation of meals.

At 40, Hajra was an energetic and organized housekeeper and a good cook. Her *biryanis*, fish curries, *khitchda* and *muthias* were well known amongst community and friends. She was particular about the right ingredients and would never proceed with making a dish unless all the required items were at hand. Surprisingly though, despite her bustling energy and culinary talents, Hajra lacked self-confidence. She had a nervous and superstitious nature. Unsure of herself, a constant worrier prone to bouts of anxiety and self-doubt, she always relied on the validation and support of those around her. But right now, time was rushing ahead and Hajra had to press on with getting the afternoon lunch ready and packed. Abdul, the young assistant from the shop would soon be there to pick up Jan Mohammed's lunch after which he would stop by at the other partner's home where he would collect a similar tiffin box with Jamshedji's lunch.

Jamshedji and his wife Mehroo, along with about twenty-five Parsee families, lived in the Camp area of Bhuj, not far from the premises occupied by Jan & Co. Their home was a good-sized bungalow with five rooms surrounded by a large balcony in the front as well as on both sides of the house. It was tastefully decorated with a carved wooden screen in the large central hall running the length of the bungalow and separating the sitting room area from the dining room behind it.

One wall of the sitting room was covered with a large tapestry depicting a pastoral scene from the English countryside whilst the opposite wall had a large portrait of Queen Victoria occupying pride of place in the centre and surrounded by family photographs on either side. Below the portrait was a showcase with several porcelain and lace figurines from Dresden and on the opposite side a comfortable sofa and chairs with antimacassars covering the arms and headrests. The coffee table in the centre and small teapoys placed between the sofa and chairs had dainty and quaint looking lace doilies. In the far corner of the sitting room was a Steinway piano and the well-worn sheet music was proof that the piano was being played regularly by one or other family member, in this case, Jamshedji's wife Mehroo.

Mehroo was a tall and slim woman in her mid-thirties, always elegantly turned out in pretty dresses or traditional Parsee style *sarees* as the occasion demanded. She was fond of jewellery and matching accessories and fine perfumes and whenever she passed by a room she left behind the lasting aroma of her sweet presence.

Jamshedji on the other hand was the exact physical opposite of his wife. Portly, with a slightly protruding belly for one who was just forty years of age, he had a clean-shaven and cherubic looking pink complexion. Good natured and with a ready smile, he had an impish sense of humour with which he chaffed his friends and those close to him. A bon vivant who loved good food and the finer things in life, he had a gramophone and an enviable collection of western classical music records and never missed his glass of port wine after a good dinner.

Unlike her husband's warm and engaging personality, Mehroo on the other hand was a bit aloof and not easily approachable. This tendency on her part did not make things easy for the self-conscious Hajra and the two women had not been able to establish the kind of friendly bond that their husbands enjoyed.

At 10 AM sharp, Jan Mohammed arrived at the shop to find Abdul the shop assistant waiting for him at the doorstep. Whichever of the two partners arrived at the store first, it was up to him to open shop. Today Jan Mohammed having arrived first, had scored over Jamshedji and he pulled out a large iron key ring from which dangled three long keys. He handed the key ring to Abdul who bent down to open the two massive pad locks on either side of a steel roller shutter. Having opened the two pad locks and relocked them in their respective hooks, Abdul lifted the handle of the shutter upwards and it went up with a loud fluttering sound revealing a thick wooden entrance door and two glass shop windows on either side.

The two decorated windows at Jan & Co. were a beholder's delight. The window on the right had a blue and white willow pattern Staffordshire dinner set with its oblong platters, serving bowls, soup bowls and dinner plates tastefully arranged and displayed. The left-hand side window had an exquisite Aynsley tea set in pure white with pink roses and green leaf borders, with unusually shaped tea cups and pretty handles. Abdul turned the key and pushed open the entrance door and the two of them entered the shop to be greeted from behind by a resounding "Good morning, Jan. I see that you have beaten me to it today." Jan Mohammed accepted the compliment from his jolly-natured partner and they both settled down to the day's business.

There were the usual requests for tableware and cutlery from the officers' mess, from the home of the British Resident or from the houses of the affluent and more westernized sections of Indian society. But today was a particularly busy day, with the visit of Mr. Stevens the majordomo from the Prag Mahal Palace.

The Prag Mahal Palace was the Bhuj residence of the *Maharao* of Kutcch, his highness Khengarji III of the Jadeja Rajput Dynasty which ruled the princely state of Kutcch from 1540 to 1948. The palace was designed in the Italian Gothic Style and was made of Italian marble and sandstone from Rajasthan with a 45-foot-high clock tower from where one could get a view of the entire Bhuj city.

The palace had been commissioned in 1865 by the previous ruler, Rao Pragmalji II who had died in 1875 before the completion of the palace. Construction was completed only in1879 during the regency of his son Khengarji III who had succeeded him on his death. A few months after reaching majority, he had been invested with full ruling powers on 14th November 1884 and in the following years he had become a popular ruler both amongst his own people as well as amongst the ruling elite in Delhi and London.

For Jan & Co. Mr. Stevens had placed a special and very large order of bone china crockery, porcelain dinnerware and decorative silverware for at the palace, hectic preparations were underway for the forthcoming birthday of his highness. A grand banquet was being planned to celebrate his 22nd birthday and visiting dignitaries from far and wide were expected at the palace to honour the young Maharao.

A New Ship Sets Sail

For the transport of their merchandise from Bombay, the partners of Jan & Co. depended on the port city of Mandvi, 60 km south of Bhuj. Mandvi had once been an important and prosperous maritime trade and shipbuilding centre and an embarkation point for pilgrimages to Mecca. But since the middle of the 19th century its importance had been eclipsed by the growing prominence of Bombay. Still, it served as an important port for all passenger and cargo steamers plying between Bhuj and Bombay. Jan Mohammed and Jamshedji took turns at making the journey to Bombay and since both partners had family connections there, they usually combined their business trips with a chance to visit their families.

The latter part of the 19th century saw the advent of steamships or steamers, and these steel-made ships fitted with steam engines now began replacing sailing ships. At Mandvi shipbuilding activity continued, but was confined to sailing ships and smaller wooden ships. The large steam powered vessels were being built overseas at ship yards owned by British shipbuilding companies. One such company was the

Grangemouth Dockyard Co. Ltd. located at Grangemouth in Scotland. Grangemouth had a fine harbour and a busy shipping trade facilitated by the construction of the Forth and Clyde Canal and offered innumerable employment opportunities to the local population.

Bruce Campbell was an ambitious and adventurous young man employed by Grangemouth Dockyard Co. to work at its shipbuilding yard where work on its first steamship project had begun in 1885. The new ship was to be 170.1 feet long, 26.5 feet broad and 9.9 feet deep with a single funnel, two masts and compound steam engines generating 73 Horsepower and a speed of 13 knots. It was an ambitious project and work conditions at the yard were demanding and tough. But Bruce Campbell was of a happy disposition and had a capacity for hard work and he had over the years been appreciated by his superiors and well-liked by his co-workers. By the time the work on the ship was completed in three years and it was ready to be launched in 1888, word got around that the company was interviewing candidates for deck hands required for the new ship.

The spirit of adventure and discovery was aroused in Bruce and he received the news with excitement. The following Sunday after church, he met up with Grace, his childhood sweetheart, at their usual place of rendezvous behind the churchyard. It had only been a week since their last meeting but for Grace the week had passed slowly and she rushed up to meet Bruce with eager anticipation. He was the centre of her universe and she adored him with a child-like devotion that was touching. Bruce was loving and protective in return and proudly boasted to his mates that Grace was the most beautiful girl in the county. Grace did pose a pretty picture with her peaches and cream complexion and cornflower blue eyes as she stood before him in a dark blue full-length tartan skirt, floral printed white blouse, light blue vest and matching blue shawl pinned to her breast with an attractive maroon brooch.

Bruce was wondering about an appropriate time to tell her about the newly completed ship and its maiden voyage to Bombay. Grace had brought along a picnic basket and she spread out a blanket under the shade of a large tree and the two enjoyed a lunch of sandwiches and mince pies washed down with apple cider. After lunch they walked arm-in-arm along the banks of the river Forth and Bruce holding Grace close to him told her about his plan to apply for the job as ship hand for the forthcoming voyage to Bombay.

Grace burst into tears and clung closer, "You're not going to leave me then, are you Bruce?"

It took Bruce a considerable amount of reassurance and cajoling, "Now, now my love 'tis only a matter of six months and I will be back and we shall be married. Think of all the grand presents that I will bring back for you from India. There will be pearls, gold and silver, and silk for your adornment." Grace smiled happily and wiped away her tears, but only after extracting from Bruce a date for their wedding fixed for the coming year. Bruce was relieved and confidently applied for and was selected to join the ship's company.

The new ship was launched and christened the "SS Vaitarna" after the river Vaitarna in the Bombay Presidency. She set sail for Bombay under the captainship of Mr. Patrick Willis, travelling around the traditional route around Africa. She docked first at Karachi and from there she proceeded to the busy port of Bombay to be handed over to its new owner Haji Kasam Ibrahim, a Kutcchi Memon aristocrat who had his office at Abdul Rehman Street and lived at Malabar Hill. She now came under the management of the "Bombay Steamer Navigation Company". This operating company had earlier engaged a crew of about forty to man the ship and had also appointed booking agents at Bhuj, Mandvi, Dwarka and Porbander. With this the SS Vaitarna was ready to start operations ferrying passengers and goods between Bombay and Mandvi and back, a sea voyage usually covered in 30 hours each way.

A Celebration and a Historical Milestone

Not surprisingly, the monsoon in Bhuj that year had been scant and unpredictable and July and August had been sweltering. With the hot, semi-arid almost desert-like climate, conditions in the old walled city with its small, narrow and winding streets could often be suffocating. Bare-chested artisans worked under such torrid conditions in tiny workshops making *ajrakh* shawls and quilts, mirror work textiles, lacquered pottery, wooden decorative carvings, or silver and gold beaten sheets for filigree and *zari* embroidery. The city walls and the city gates had been repeatedly damaged and rebuilt after the 1819 earthquake and evidence of the patchwork reconstruction could be seen all around.

Kanti Desai, who worked as the accountant and bookkeeper at Jan & Co, lived in the old walled city. Whereas most of the houses here were single storey stone structures, Kanti's house was a handsome, double storey building made of heavy timber with an ornate and artistic doorway which made his home stand out from amongst its neighbours in the main vegetable market area in the heart of the old city.

Kanti Desai would leave home early on foot in order to be in time at the shop since both Jan Mohammed and Jamshedji were sticklers for punctuality. However, Kanti was a dedicated and gifted accountant and a wizard with figures and the partners often turned the Nelson's eye when he occasionally arrived late. Jan Mohammed in fact was particularly indulgent with Kanti because in his father's tradition he was always game for an amusing story and Kanti had a stock of funny anecdotes which he would sometimes dare to relate in front of his bosses if he found them in a good mood. Today seemed to be a good day because business had been thriving and the atmosphere prevailing at the shop was jovial and light-hearted.

"Sir, would you like to hear the story about my friend who went down to the river to bathe?" Kanti offered tentatively.

"Yes, yes please go ahead," encouraged Jan Mohammed. Kanti had been waiting for an excuse to tell his latest joke and he began,

"On a hot summer's day my friend decided to go down to the river to bathe. He was in the process of undressing and piling up his clothes behind a large rock on the river's bank, when he heard a voice calling, 'Hey Bhola.' He cocked up his ears and looked around to see who the one calling out was, but he could see no one. He dismissed the voice and went ahead towards the river. Hardly had he stepped into the water than he heard the voice again, 'Arre oh, Bhola'. He looked around desperately here and there but he could see no one. Once again, he ignored the voice and walked deeper into the river. Now with the water waist-deep he heard the voice for a third time, 'Oh, ho Bhola.' Frustrated and exasperated he turned around this time, ran up to the river bank and with arms held akimbo shouted in an irritated voice, "How many times must I tell you that my name is not Bhola?"

Both Jan Mohammed and Jamshedji burst out laughing. Now in the same relaxed and happy frame of mind, Jamshedji teased, "What surprise do you have for me today, Jan?" as Abdul set out their lunch in the small back room behind the shop. The partners shared an easy camaraderie and often shared each other's lunch and today Jamshedji eyed Jan Mohammed's spicy fish curry and *moong dal khichdi* with a mischievous glint in his eyes. Jan Mohammed readily shared his own lunch and in exchange relished Jamshedji's *sali boti* and *bhida par eidoo*.

On the 4th of September it was going to be the fifth anniversary of the establishment of their company. With a healthy balance sheet, the partners had planned a small celebration. Unknown at the time, the 4th of September 1888 was to mark another milestone in the broader context of the country's history. On this day the young Mohandas Karamchand Gandhi set sail from Bombay for England to pursue his law studies in London, launching a career that was to have a far-reaching impact on the future of his country.

The celebration was in the form of a pot luck dinner at Jamshedji and Mehroo's house. Hajra, conscious of her limited and faltering English and not being comfortable in mixed company, had not wanted to go and it required a lot of persuasion on the part of Jan Mohammed before she reluctantly agreed to accompany him. The hosts had also invited an English couple, Major Colin White and his wife Catherine. Unlike a lot of English officers and their wives who kept to themselves and did not socialize with the local Indian community in Bhuj, Major White and his wife had Indian friends and mixed freely amongst the local population. They had first come into contact with Jamshedji as customers who had strolled in one day at Jan & Co. looking to purchase a porcelain dinner set. Their friendship had developed further on the premises of the St. Joseph's School, a British style boy's school established in Bhuj in the year 1870. Again, unlike many of their fellow countrymen, Major White and his wife had not sent off their son Patrick for studies to England but had enrolled him at St. Joseph's School. This was the school where Jamshedji also sent his son Behram and the two boys finding themselves in the same class, had become close friends and shared a common passion for football.

At the small dinner party, Hajra had brought along mince *samosas* and her famous *khichda* - a traditional Muslim dish made with rice, lentils, cubes of mutton and spices. Mehroo had made *patra ni macchi* - steamed fish and chutney in banana leaves and *lagan nu custard* as dessert whilst Catherine had contributed a shepherd's pie and an orange soufflé. All put together it made a veritable feast and everyone relished the food. When they sat down with their coffees, Major White, noticing the piano in the corner asked, "Who in the family plays the piano? Do we get to hear a demonstration of your musical talents?"

Mehroo blushed and replied modestly, "Oh I am just learning to play." However, with a little nudging from her husband, she obliged and played a charming piece from a piano solo. Everyone applauded appreciatively and the evening ended with the Whites proposing a dinner at their house the next time. Going back home in their carriage, Hajra rested her head on Jan Mohammed's shoulder, held his hand and thanked him. Having overcome her inhibitions, she had in fact enjoyed the evening.

The buoyant mood in Jan Mohammed's household was further enhanced by the news from Bombay. The parents had learnt from a letter they had received the previous week that Aisha was happy and comfortable in Bombay and had been enjoying her stay there, attending community functions and events in the company of her aunt. Hajra began to wonder if her apprehensions about leaving Aisha behind in Bombay had after all been unwarranted, until an incident occurred the following month that brought back her anxiety, gave her sleepless nights and destroyed her peace of mind.

A Cryptic Prophecy

On a Thursday afternoon in October, Hajra was readying herself for an engagement ceremony she had to attend at the home of a friend. Kutcchi Memon alliances usually began with a bit of matchmaking done by the elders of the community and culminated by a formal proposal from the boy's side. The male family members from both sides would then meet between themselves to formalize and seal the engagement and sweet refreshments would be passed around. This was followed by an exclusive ladies event called a *bolani* where the young bride to be was given a gift of clothing and jewellery from the boy's side including sometimes an engagement ring. With Kutcchi Memons, engagements and marriages tended to be endogamous, within the same community or group with common social values and customs.

As she began getting dressed, Hajra's thoughts automatically drifted towards her own daughter. The time was now ripe when she and Jan Mohammed would have to start thinking of a suitable match for Aisha. How and when this would occur would have to be left in God's hands.

But she knew that as parents they would have to in some manner initiate the process. Dressed in the traditional long ankle length gown and pyjamas with embroidered bottoms and a *bandhni odhni*, Hajra nonetheless had to cover herself fully with her heavy gold embroidered *milaya* and *missar* scarf before she could step out of the house and walk the short distance to the home of her friend.

She was about to step out of the house when she heard a loud cry emanating from outside the verandah steps. "*Bibi, Allah ke naam par kuch dedo*". (Lady, give alms. God will bless you.) The voice came from a mendicant fakir who would come by erratically now and then but particularly on Thursdays to seek food and alms. He had a flowing white beard and kohl darkened eyelids and was dressed in a long loose fitting black *abaya* and a green turban with several layers of beads strung around his neck. He wore copious silver rings capped with coloured stones on the fingers of both hands. In one hand he held a long *tasbih* and in the other a deep begging bowl.

Hajra was used to his occasional presence by her verandah steps and would often ask Aisha to fetch food from the kitchen and put it out onto his begging bowl. This along with a small donation in cash was readily accepted and would be followed by a long litany of blessings for the health and happiness of all the family members. This Thursday was no exception and Hajra herself doled out the food and alms. The fakir, noticing the absence of Aisha, asked after her and being told she was away, exclaimed "Go to her now Bibi, or you will never see her again." With this he turned around and disappeared, leaving Hajra dumbfounded and stunned.

A Young Sailor's Misadventures

For Bruce Campbell the five-month long journey to Bombay had been both eventful and rewarding. The long hours of watch on the bridge had been lonely and he missed Grace terribly, but he was grateful for the experience he had gained as a first-time sailor and was looking forward to collecting his wages on reaching port.

With the coming of steamships and later with the opening of the Suez Canal in 1870, England was brought closer and the trade between India and England began to expand by leaps and bounds. The landscape of Bombay harbour began to change dramatically and the entire water-front from Colaba to Mazgaon was soon lined by wharfs, docks and godowns. In the late 19th century, the Wellington Pier, better known by its popular local name of "Apollo Bunder", was an important pier for embarkation and disembarkation of passengers and goods from the ships arriving in Bombay. It was only later in the year 1900 that the British administration started to reclaim the area in order to build the Gateway of India, to welcome King George V and Queen Mary on their arrival in India in 1911.

In order to get a passage back to London and onward from there to Grangemouth, Scotland, Bruce would have to wait a few days at Bombay. So, he decided to check into a small hotel in the Colaba area and utilize the extra few days to explore Bombay.

In the year 1888, as our young adventurer set out to discover Bombay it had already started taking its first strides towards becoming a 'modern' city. Remarkable transformations were taking place. The roads were becoming wider and lit by gas lamps that had started being installed since 1865. Bombay had become an attractive city, not merely a prosperous one with imposing public buildings especially in the Fort Area which gave the locality a dignified and stately appearance: The Secretariat building and the High Court, and in the University area the Convocation Hall and the Rajabai Tower.

But there were other less attractive aspects to the growing city as Bruce was to find out to his chagrin. After an early dinner that first evening, he stepped out of his hotel to take a stroll along the waterfront not far from where he was staying. He had decided that the following day he would venture into the commercial districts of the city to buy the few items he had promised to take back for Grace. But for now, he enjoyed the balmy evening air as he walked through the small streets leading to the pier.

A shadowy figure with several broken teeth and a twisted mouth limped across to him and mumbled something into his ear, "*Sahib, Sahib, Chinese hai Chinese*". Bruce did not understand what he was trying to convey and he countered, "Sorry mate what did you say?" The man appeared to have plucked up some courage and he crept a little closer,

"Sahib, Chinese girl, very nice. You will like." With a rush of anger and disgust, Bruce managed to figure out what he was implying and very nearly cuffed him a hard blow to his twisted mouth, but instead he quickened his pace and rushed ahead.

The following morning Bruce set out to check out the bazaars of Bombay. For getting around the city he had a variety of transport options from horse-drawn *shigrams* and bullock-drawn *reklas* to horse-drawn *victorias* and even one and two horse-drawn tram cars. Curious about the tram cars, Bruce asked around and decided to jump on to the next available tramcar which was crowded with tightly packed passengers sitting on wooden bench-type seats. As the tram pulled by two sturdy horses surged forward Bruce had to hold on tightly to the footboard where he had barely managed to secure a footing. It was a long and slow ride with the tram driver having to frequently alert passing vehicles and pedestrians to clear the way by pressing his foot down on a round pedal which emitted a clanging metallic chime. The tram reached the terminus at Bori Bunder where the horses were watered and changed before the tram continued on its way. Bruce had by now managed to get a seat but he was glad when the tram finally reached its destination.

The Crawford Market, named after Arthur Crawford, the first Municipal Commissioner of the city, was completed in 1869, and in 1882, the building was the first in India to be lit up by electricity. It was the centre of market life in South Bombay and was the main wholesale market for fruit, vegetables and poultry. Apart from Crawford Market, there were three main bazaars in south Bombay that were linked through a network of serpentine crossroads. The streets were crowded with a jumble of vendors, coolies and carts, and the sanitary conditions here were unhygienic with poorly developed civic amenities. But these bazaars were laden with a colourful and exotic variety of goods from silk and cotton fabrics, silver and gold jewellery, antiques, spices and a host of other items displayed by stalls or street vendors lining both sides of the narrow lanes. Bruce being a careful shopper decided to make an investigative tour and to come back the following day to make his final purchases. But fate had other plans in store for him.

On his return to the bazaars on his third day in the city, he stopped by a cloth merchant to select and pay for a length of silk that he had chosen to take back for Grace. Imagine his shock and dismay as he reached for his purse to find that it was missing. Instead there was a neat slit in the lining of the pocket in which he had carried all the balance money from his wages. In the melee of the crowded bazaar he had been robbed by a wily and light-fingered pickpocket. Distraught, empty-handed and penniless, he trudged back to his hotel exhausted.

Alone and with no one to turn to he could only think of the ship's captain and the shipping company that had taken over operations in Bombay. Fortunately for him they were sympathetic to his predicament and he was offered lodgings and a position as crew member of the SS Vaitarna that was going to set sail for Mandvi in a week's time. For Bruce what was going to be a brief stopover of a few days in Bombay, was turning out to be an extended adventure. Or was it...?

A Passage to Bombay is Booked

Horrified by the Fakir's ominous prediction, Hajra slumped down into the nearest chair. A cold shiver ran down her back and she sat motionless staring blankly at the empty space in front of her. What had he meant when he said that they would never see their daughter again? Was she in some imminent danger? Was there some horrible misfortune that awaited her? Should she and her husband rush to Bombay as soon as possible to be by her side? Was there still enough time or was it already too late? These and other morbid thoughts plagued her mind and she could find no peace. At length she forced herself to go back inside the house and change into her usual home clothes. She would somehow have to explain her absence at the engagement ceremony to her friend, but for now she waited impatiently for her husband to return home.

Jan Mohammed found his wife disturbed and extremely agitated as she tearfully described to him the events of that afternoon. Fearing for her daughter's safety and wellbeing she implored, "Sait let us go off to Bombay as soon as a ship is available to take us there. I am extremely worried about Aisha and want to be with her." Jan Mohammed listened patiently and gently soothed and comforted his wife although he did not believe in the pointless utterances of fakirs and found that his wife's fears were irrational. However, without ever openly admitting it, he also missed his gentle and loving daughter, and promised Hajra that he would have a word with his business partner and make enquiries about the next ship sailing for Bombay.

The following day, true to his word, Jan Mohammed discussed his plans for visiting Bombay with his partner citing a family matter that required his and his wife's presence in Bombay forthwith. Jamshedji was understanding and since Jan Mohammed's business trip to Bombay was due anyway the following month, he found there was no reason why he could not go a month earlier.

In fact, he teased good-humouredly, "I am sure there is a promising proposal for Aisha's hand from a bright young man in Bombay." Jan Mohammed smiled without elaborating further, thanked Jamshedji for his co-operation and left the shop early that evening.

At home Jan Mohammed saw that his wife had been waiting anxiously for his return and he was quick to give her the good news. He had spoken to his partner Jamshedji who had been very supportive. Moreover, a new ship called the SS Vaitarna was due to arrive at Mandvi port in the next one week and the ship operators had started accepting bookings for passengers wishing to travel to Bombay. The new steamer was modern in design with three floors and twenty-five cabins and he had secured a cabin booking for the two of them. The ship was due to sail for Bombay on 8th November. Jan Mohammed also informed his wife that that very afternoon he had sent off a letter to his cousin Rehman informing him of their forthcoming trip to Bombay.

Hajra was happy and relieved at receiving the news and had regained some of her composure.

Although she was still sleeping badly and suffered from bouts of anxiety, the anticipation of seeing her daughter again had helped allay some of her initial fears. She also shared with Jan Mohammed her view that it was time that they starting looking for a suitable match for Aisha, perhaps by putting in a word to relatives in Bombay. He agreed with her and also told her what Jamshedji had jokingly suggested. Although it was still premature with no proposal on the horizon just as yet, both parents were taken up with the idea that efforts needed to be made in this direction. Hajra said she was intending to consult her sister on putting together items for Aisha's wedding trousseau whilst she was in Bombay and Jan Mohammed, in spite of himself, let slip that he had ordered from one of his English suppliers a complete bone china tea service which he had intended to be a wedding present for their daughter. It was to be delivered before the yearend to Rehman in Bombay. With these dreamy plans both parents were looking forward contentedly to be reunited with their daughter after a gap of six months.

Disaster Strikes at Sea

The SS Vaitarna arrived at Mandvi Port on 5th November 1888. As news spread about its arrival a lot of interest and excitement was generated around the giant new ship and throngs of curious bystanders gathered on the pier side to view and admire the vessel. Instead of its official name it began to be referred to by the popular nickname of "Vijli" or electricity since it was lighted with electric bulbs, a novel feature for the time.

Hajra had busied herself for the past several days preparing foodstuffs that she knew were Aisha's favourites and also well-liked by other members of the family. She packed and stacked away boxes and tins filled with *gur papdi, roat, pakwan, nankhatais* and *khajuris*. Not knowing how long they were going to be away, she had sent off Sakina to her village with a month's advance pay. For his part Jan Mohammed spent the next few days making a careful inventory of the stocks in the shop, making notes for the items for which he needed to place fresh indents and identifying agents in Bombay with whom he would have to renegotiate contracts for the coming year. Of late at Jan &

Co. they had also been stocking items sourced from local artisans in the old walled city. Silver ornamental pieces, wood carved items and lacquer work had moved quite well and he reminded Jamshedji that fresh orders needed to be placed for these goods.

Jan Mohammad and Hajra had had to leave Bhuj early the previous day to make the 60 km ride to Mandvi and had availed themselves of the hospitality of Kanti Desai's brother Vitthaldas and his family for their overnight stay there. Because of the rapport between Jan Mohammed and Kanti, his brother Vitthaldas had not hesitated to welcome Jan Mohammed to his home. That apart, it was also widely acknowledged that Kutcchi merchants both Hindu and Muslim interacted and co-operated well with each other and that religious or caste differences did not hamper relationships between them. In fact, cultural synthesis and a blending of religious rituals and practices was a feature of Kutcchi culture with Hindu saints as well as Muslim *pirs* being commonly revered by members of both communities.

From the beginning of the 19th century Mandvi had become an important textile production centre and there was a thriving export trade to Africa and Arabia. Vitthaldas traded in both fine and coarse cotton cloth destined primarily for African markets. His home was located in a busy and crowded by-lane in the commercial area of Mandvi located at a short distance behind the port. It was a two-storey building with his shop occupying the ground floor with the residential quarters housed on the upper floors. Vitthaldas and his wife Ansuya occupied the first floor, whilst the second floor was taken up by their married son and his family.

Dinner that evening was a delicious Gujarati vegetarian meal and Ansuya served up an array of different dishes arranged in gleaming silver *thalis*. To begin with there were snack-type items such as *dhoklas* and *patras* with a spicy green chutney and a sweet and sour tamarind chutney offering a tantalizing mixture of sweet and spicy that was meant to tickle the taste buds. Next, she dished out portions of stir-fried vegetables such as eggplant, ladyfinger and spinach eaten with *bhakhri*, a round, flat unleavened homemade bread. This was followed by fluffy white rice with *kadhi*, a thick gravy made of chickpea flour and yogurt and served with fried *pakoras*. Hajra attempted to protest, "You should not have taken so much trouble, *behen*." "It is no trouble at all," countered Ansuya, "We are honoured to have you as our guests and I hope that you have enjoyed our simple, home-made vegetarian food." Jan Mohammed assured her that it had been a veritable feast and the meal ended with two types of sweet dishes – *shrikhand* and *doodhpak*, one being yogurt based and the other milk based. Before retiring for the night Jan Mohammed and Hajra thanked their hosts and said how much they had missed having Kanti with them that evening.

The next morning Vitthaldas and Ansuya accompanied them to the pier to bid farewell and see off their guests. Arriving at the dock they found the area busy and animated with a large number of marriage parties bound for Bombay carrying large trunks filled with bridal finery and festival clothing, sundry decorative arrangements and boxes of freshly prepared food items. Along with the large number of marriage invitees there was also a fully equipped Gujarati musical band. Running hither and thither trying to get a last-minute passage was a motley group of students headed to Bombay to appear for the matriculation examination. Amongst the other passengers waiting to board were some small family groups, a mix of British and Indian businessmen, army men and even a doctor or two.

The SS Vaitarna left Mandvi port on Thursday 8th November at 12 noon with 520 passengers and 43 crew members. She reached the port of Dwarka where she picked up a further 183 passengers taking the total passenger number to 703. She left for Porbander but due to bad weather she did not stop at Porbander and headed directly for Bombay, a port that she would never reach.

Late that evening she encountered a heavy cyclonic storm with high, gusty winds with speeds of 100 miles per hour and over. The strong winds were accompanied by torrential rain and storm surges that caused gigantic waves to rise high above the surface of the sea lashing the sides of the ship and repeatedly sending it tossing upwards only to come crashing down again in a mad seesaw. Mayhem reigned on board the ship. The screams of the terrified women and children could be heard above the crashing waves as they sat huddled together, drenched to the bone and desperately clutching each other's wet bodies. As the ship swayed relentlessly upwards and downwards some clung on for dear life to whatever firm object they could lay their hands on only to be dragged cruelly away by the sheer force of the wind and the rain. The harried crew members tried frantically to garner all possible help to the panic stricken and helpless passengers. But hampered by the ferocity of nature, their efforts were rendered useless. Being ill-equipped to handle a tempest of such a devastating magnitude, the SS Vaitarna was overpowered and after a valiant battle with the stormy sea she was sadly wrecked and sank off the coast near Mangrol. The hopes and dreams of the 750 people on board were shattered and their lives snuffed out in the matter of a few hours.

The next day the ship was declared missing. The Bombay Presidency and the shipping companies sent out steamers to find the wreckage. But there were no survivors. No wreckage, no debris and no bodies were ever found. The ship had just mysteriously vanished and the bodies of all its passengers and crew consigned to a watery grave.

After the disaster, a number of questions and theories were put forth on the ship's seaworthiness and whether adequate safety measures had been put in place. Did it have enough lifeboats and life jackets on board? Had there been any instance of foul play or a conspiracy of some kind? Was this a case involving the hand of the supernatural and in the case of Jan Mohammed and Hajra, had they been pushed to their deaths by the cryptic prophecy of an itinerant fakir? The questions and doubts remained unanswered.

Unbearable Grief and Then a Healing Touch

News of the shipwreck and the disappearance of Vijli was slow to reach the families in Gujarat and Bombay. When it did finally get to them, it was met with shock and utter disbelief. Throngs of people gathered at Rehman and Halima's home to offer their condolences and there were the usual prayers for the departed offered both at the mosque and at ladies' gatherings at the house. But Aisha was devastated. Her cries of anguish pierced through the house and no words of comfort or the unequivocal outpourings of her aunt's love could console her or assuage her grief. She began to shun the company of others, became silent and depressed and withdrew deeper into her shell. She would sit for hours by the window in her room staring at the empty sky until the fading light of the setting sun cast deep shadows over the roof tops of the surrounding buildings. Sometimes she would look down to the street below and see the lamp lighter on his daily sunset rounds armed with his tall ladder as he went around from street to street lighting up the gas lit lamp posts in his locality.

The steady stream of sympathisers and well-wishers, and the letters and messages of condolence continued to pour in. The 40th day, marking the official close of the mourning period, arrived and went by. Aisha remained locked in her grief, until one day towards the end of December, Rehman announced that a consignment of goods had arrived in Aisha's name from the distant shores of England. It was the bone china tea service that her father had ordered for her. It was a beautiful blue and gold lined set of the finest egg shell china with six dainty cups and saucers, a large and elegantly shaped tea pot, milk jug and sugar bowl and half a dozen dessert bowls and an equal number of side plates.

Aisha was overwhelmed by the arrival of this unexpected, posthumous gift from her parents. Her spirits lifted as she felt engulfed by their presence around her and she carefully picked up and fondled each piece. Where other attempts to console her had failed, this symbol of her parents' great love for her, finally brought her the comfort and solace that she had so far blocked out. Gradually over the following weeks the colour began to appear back on Aisha's face and she started participating in the family's activities. Orphaned at the age of 16 years, the void left by the loss of her parents remained with her throughout her life. But with the unstinting love and support of her family she began to face life with more equanimity and a kind of resigned peace now descended upon her.

The same could not be said for poor, hapless Grace, the waiting bride-to-be in distant Scotland. Grace was in total denial and refused to accept the story of the ship's disappearance. She stubbornly insisted that it was only time before her Bruce would return and the two of them would be married. Some said that she had lost her mind as she was spotted endlessly scanning the horizon from a clifftop for signs of a returning ship or wandering aimlessly amongst the fields of purple heather. Until one day her blue shawl was washed ashore on the rocks below the cliff at Grangemouth. It was presumed that she had plunged to her death in a bid to be reunited with her beloved Bruce deep within the ocean's depths.

The Aftermath

The mourning period for Jan Mohammed and Hajra over, Aisha's cousins Rehana and Rizwana tried to encourage Aisha to go out on outings with them. She would join them sometimes after much coaxing but preferred to remain indoors. Always shy and slightly withdrawn, she would at times appear to be far away and lost in a world of her own thoughts. Halima bore an unflinching love for her sixteen-year-old niece, much to the envy of her own daughters. She understood Aisha's temperament better than anyone and she had long ago decided that at times like this it was best to leave Aisha to herself. After the tragic loss of her parents, the move to Bombay from her native Bhuj had been thrust upon her and she needed to adjust to her new surroundings. Given time and understanding Aisha would sooner or later return to the world around her.

In Bhuj, Kanti Desai's eyes would well up with tears as he thought fondly of Jan Mohammed. He missed the excellent relationship he had shared with him, more as an equal than as a boss and the occasional light-hearted moments he had enjoyed in his company on account of his penchant for exchanging funny stories. He thought ruefully of the fact that it had been his brother and not himself who had had the chance to see off Jan Mohammed and his wife at the pier at Mandvi before their fateful departure.

As for Jamshedji, he never quite recovered from the loss of his partner and friend Jan Mohammed. The memory of the close bond that he had shared with him and the happy times they had spent together both in and out of the shop continued to haunt him. He tried listlessly to run the business on his own for a few years. His son Behram had moved to Bombay for further studies and subsequently for medical studies to London. Now a successful doctor with a clinic in Harley Street he had asked his parents to join him in London. Jamshedji eventually wound up Jan & Co. and he and his wife sailed for London but not before he had justly and equitably settled Aisha's inheritance upon her. Unfortunately for Aisha, Jan Mohammed's house in Bhuj had been totally wrecked in the earthquake that hit Bhuj in October 1898.

Life in Halima's household continued as usual. On the eve of the holy month of Ramadan, Halima and the girls went up to the roof of their house to sight the nascent crescent moon ushering the beginning of the new month. The period of fasting and prayer would begin the next day when the entire household would rise an hour and a half before sunrise to partake the pre-dawn *sehri* meal. For the three girls staying without food and drink throughout the day was not the most exacting part of the fast, it was being roused from deep sleep at three or four in the morning which was the most challenging.

Rehana was the lazy one, "Oh, I am just getting up" she would mumble with sleep-heavy eyelids and promptly go back to sleep. For her sleep was paramount and she would protest to her mother, "Can't I just keep a glass of milk by my bedside, gulp it down quickly and go back to sleep?"

But Halima would have none of it and would send Rizwana to forcibly drag Rehana out of bed. She would grudgingly creep out of bed and would be the last at table. Aisha on the other hand, had by now adapted herself to her new set-up, and felt a deep sense of indebtedness towards her aunt. She would wake up early and on her own and would be standing beside Halima helping her with the preparations. Beloved of her parents as she had been, she had not been spoilt by them and her mother Hajra had from an early age involved her in helping with the cooking and the household chores.

The meal would soon be over and the last drink of water taken before the crier with his drum would be out declaring for all to hear that the time for *sehri* was past. This would be followed a few minutes later by the call of the muezzin summoning the faithful to the dawn prayer. Rehman would go down to the nearby mosque to offer his prayers whilst the ladies would stand together and pray at home. After the prayers everyone would get into bed and try to catch some sleep.

The days of the fast were long, especially in the summer months and the evening *ifthaar* or breaking of the fast would be eagerly awaited. The fast was always broken first with some dates and a drink either of water or some sweet sherbet or fruit juice, followed by fresh cut fruit and some snack items such as *samosas* or *pakoras*. After the evening prayers and a short gap, Halima would serve a light dinner. An all-time favourite was *haleem* followed by a dessert such as *phirni* or a milk based *halwa* set with china grass and cut into neat diamond shaped pieces and topped with a sprinkling of nuts. After dinner, Rehman would rush off to the mosque for the special night prayer of *taraweeh* recited in congregation during the month of Ramadan.

And so, the months and years slipped by. In July 1895 a proposal came to Rehman and Halima asking for the hand in marriage of Rehana and Rizwana for two Kutcchi Memon brothers whose family was settled in Mauritius. The parents were flattered and overjoyed for their two daughters and after making relevant enquiries about the background and status of the family in question, agreed to the proposal. Since the grooms and their families were abroad and were coming to Bombay for only a limited period of time, the engagement was followed almost immediately by a charming joint wedding ceremony for the two sisters married to two brothers.

Just a week after the marriage the two sisters left with their husbands and their new family for Mauritius. The parting was tearful. In all their happiness, Rehman and Halima were saddened that their daughters would now be far away from them, but found some consolation in the fact that the sisters would at least be together.

With the siblings away, Aisha and Halima were the only two women left in the house and the bond between aunt and niece grew even stronger. Demure and self-deprecating by nature, Aisha tended always to need the support of others to bolster her own self esteem. But she was quick to reciprocate love and although she took time to adapt and adjust to change, Halima was confident that with time and given the right opportunity Aisha would manage to make her own life. But time seemed to be running out. Protective as she had always been about Aisha, Halima was now getting seriously concerned about her marriage prospects as Aisha that year had turned twenty-three.

PART 2

MALEGAUM – 1886-1898

Father-Son Team of Handloom Weavers

Temporary Hospital for Plague Victims, Bombay 1896

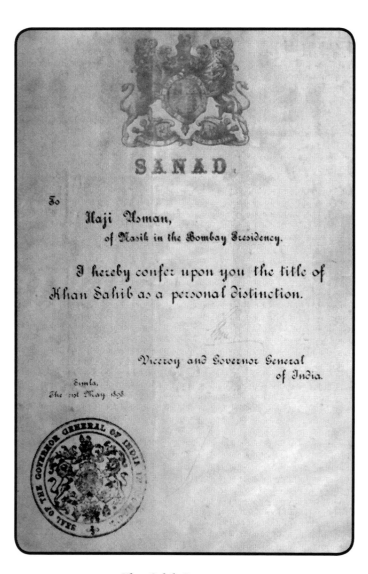

SANAD.

To

Haji Usman,
of Nasik in the Bombay Presidency.

I hereby confer upon you the title of Khan Sahib as a personal distinction.

Viceroy and Governor General
of India.

Simla,
The 21st May 1898.

Khan Sahib Citation, 1898

The Hamlet of Gardens

The migratory instinct which had prompted the earliest Momins or Memons to move out of Thatta in the 15th century, was once again evident from the first quarter of the 19th century in Kutcch when the search for wealth and commercial opportunities saw a number of Kutcchi Memons migrating outwards towards Bombay. The first Kutcchi Memon settlements in Bombay tended to be concentrated in the Mandvi and Chakla areas and families sought the comfort and security of mingling with their own kind. Later, with growing prosperity, education and exposure, they began interacting with other communities and some families moved to the more affluent and cosmopolitan areas of south Bombay.

Being an enterprising community, they entered into business and trade activities and quickly improved their standard of living and that of others of their community. They got together under the leadership of prominent and wealthy members of the community known as *Patels*. These influential community leaders also came from a tradition of sharing their wealth for the betterment of their fellows and over a period of time they made charitable donations towards the construction of community halls, places of worship, hospitals, *musafirkhanas* and schools. One such Kutcchi Memon notable was Sait Haji Usman who moved further afield to the hinterland beyond Bombay and settled in Malegaum (known today as Malegaon) in the Nasik district, located 280 km north-east of Bombay and on the road linking Bombay and Agra.

Malegaum used to be a small junction known as "Maliwadi" (hamlet of gardens) until it shot into prominence roughly back in 1740 when a local *jahagirdar*, Naro Shankar Raje Bahadur, started building a fort in the area. As the fort took 25 years to build, a sizeable number of Muslim workers and artisans from places like Surat and northern India settled in the area. Throughout the 19th century there were waves of migration from Uttar Pradesh, The Deccan and Khandesh areas and Malegaum became something of a shelter and a source of employment during times of reversals. The famine of 1862 again saw a large body of Muslims from the Varanasi area mostly weavers or *julahas* by profession move to the weaving towns of Malegaum, Ahmednagar and Bhiwandi. Malegaum being situated at the confluence of two rivers, the Girna and the Mausam, had the added advantage of good and plentiful water and it soon began to attract immigrant workers from far and wide. Overcome by poverty and dwindling employment opportunities in their original homes, they were drawn to places like Malegaum which offered attractive possibilities for those with skills. The immigration process was furthered by the phenomenon of the "kin connection." Once a particular family was reasonably well settled, word was sent back to those left back home to come join. The arrival and settlement of newer migrants was thus made possible through a family or kinship pattern that facilitated the newcomer with initial help in terms of food and shelter until he had, so to say, learnt the ropes.

Haji Usman saw a business opportunity at Malegaum but being a visionary and a capitalist with a social conscience, he also realised that the infusion of capital would contribute to the social and economic development of the region. So, in January 1886, accompanied by his wife Sara, he moved to Malegaum, and by the middle of 1888, whilst Jan Mohammed had a prosperous business running in Bhuj, Haji Usman had made considerable investments in handloom workshops and factories, land and buildings and gained for himself a position of respect and leadership amongst the weaving community of Malegaum. Unbeknownst to these two Kutcchi Memon gentlemen, unknown to each other and separated as they were by geography, the destinies of their progeny would somehow be intertwined in the years to come.

The Plight of the Migrant Weavers

Arriving in Malegaum in 1886, Haji Usman was appalled by the poverty and the poor living and working conditions of the immigrant weavers and their families. Although after agriculture, the handloom sector was the largest employment and livelihood provider to the area, the mill spun yarn and cloth from Britain had adversely impacted the production of hand-spun yarn and handloom cloth. The weavers were dependent on the procurement of yarn and dyes from rapacious middlemen and invariably found themselves in deep debt. Working long hours in badly lit and poorly ventilated sheds, often whole families were involved in eking out a subsistence level existence. The men typically worked as weavers, the women on winding and sizing operations, and children as assistants in both weaving and winding. The looms were driven either by hand or by leg or by both, often using outdated and archaic implements.

Haji Usman was determined to bring about change and to work towards the welfare and uplift of this downtrodden and exploited section of society. But for this he would need the help and support of his wife. Aged 33 and 23 respectively, they were a relatively young couple, who after four years of marriage, had not as yet been blessed with any offspring. Haji Usman was a large man, tall and well-built with an imposing personality. He had a broad face with a fleshy nose and wore a full beard and never stepped out of the house without his *kutcchi pagdi* adorning his head. Sara on the other hand, at five feet, was small made, almost diminutive. But what she lacked in physical stature, she more than made up by a strength of character and great will power. She was devoted to her husband and was ready to stand firmly by his side to support him in all matters.

They lived in relative comfort and luxury in an area east of the river Mausam in a simple but spacious one-storey, bungalow. It was an austere looking building made of stone with a stark whitewashed finish and set in a large walled compound with a garden in front and a sizeable backyard. The bungalow had a hall in the centre and rooms on each side of the hall, and a large verandah in front facing the garden. Under the porch stood a handsome two-horse carriage. The kitchen and servants' quarters were located in the back of the house where there was also a stable for the horses and a cowshed housing the two cows which supplied the household with its daily supply of fresh milk. Sara also liked keeping a brood of poultry which she fed and lovingly looked after herself. She fed them a mixture of *bajra* and other millets twice a day as the chickens ran cluck-clucking after her as she spread out the grain with the little chicks scampering hungrily after their mothers.

Sara was also an accomplished seamstress and one of the first steps that she undertook was to hold afternoon classes three times a week to teach sewing, embroidery and crochet to the women of the community. At first the women were suspicious and hesitant but they soon joined her classes in large numbers as they realised that attending the classes being held by Sara would provide them with a degree of self-reliance and the skills necessary towards earning a supplementary source of income for their families. Haji Usman fully encouraged Sara in this venture which would work side by side with his own efforts to increase employment and improve working conditions through the new weaving workshops that he had established. It was their combined efforts and team work that finally bore results.

More than two thirds of the looms were worked by Muslim migrants from North India. A few of these migrant families especially from the districts of Mau and Azamgarh in U.P., despite their *julaha* origins, had a strong background in Persian and Urdu language and literature. Similarly, some of the migrant families from the Deccan came from educated backgrounds and a few individuals from amongst them were even teachers. There was Humza for example, an extremely gifted blind person with an amazing memory and the ability to recall historical details with great accuracy. He had also committed the entire Quran to memory and become a *hafiz* and commanded great respect amongst the local population. He would hold classes to teach the young to recite the Quran and to read and write Urdu. Haji Usman made efforts to encourage and sponsor such individuals and provided the space and infrastructure through donations to encourage the spread of education within the community.

He also had an eye for spotting talent and was able to single out enthusiastic young men from amongst his workers who could be trained and moulded towards shouldering greater responsibilities and eventually becoming game changers for the community. One such promising young man he found in Aslam Khan who came from a weaving family of Mubarakpur that had seen better days in the past.

A Rising Young Star

Driven by hunger and deprivation, Aslam Khan and his family consisting of his parents and two younger sisters, had moved to Malegaum in 1873. Although newer railway connections had been introduced in North India, travel was slow and arduous and involved a combination of bullock cart, train and invariably long treks on foot. At the tender age of 11 years he had had to join his father in the handloom sheds and together father and son worked between 12 to 16 hours a day to keep the family from starvation. His father would coax him to devote some time towards the study of his books and then Aslam would stay up late at night and under the dim light of a kerosene lamp, he would pore over the text books that he had brought along with him from Mubarakpur. And so, the years passed until one day in 1888 the family's fortunes changed with the opening of one of Haji Usman's workshops in their locality.

Aslam Khan now 26 years was a sturdy young man with broad shoulders and Haji Usman saw that he was honest and industrious and showed great promise. Blessed with a naturally inquisitive mind, he impressed Haji Usman with his willingness to experiment and to learn new ideas and techniques. Haji Usman put him in charge of a team of workers and in due course Aslam was given the responsibility of supervising ten weaving workshops. His father was pleased with his progress and the improvement in their standard of living which his success had made possible. Being himself hardworking and innovative, Aslam Khan was able to set a fine example to the men working under him and to teach them newer methods and techniques.

On a hot day in June 1893, Aslam Khan was on a train journey to arrange for the purchase of imported English yarn from the yarn markets of Bombay. He had also been entrusted with the responsibility of buying new equipment and the latest weaving contraptions for the looms. In 1865, the train link from Bombay to Bhusaval had been established. But the journey from Malegaum to Bombay was slow and long. There was no railway station at Malegaum and he had to travel by bullock cart to the rail head at Manmad which was 40 odd km from Malegaum, and the journey from Manmad to Bombay involved several train stops on the way.

Having braved the rigours of a long and tortuous journey, Aslam Khan set foot in Bombay on his first ever trip to this bustling commercial hub. Even for someone well used to living by his wits, the sudden exposure to this large city and its teeming yarn market with its shoving and jostling crowds and crafty deal makers was an experience to contend with. But unfazed by the strangeness and newness of his surroundings, the young man held his own and within a few days returned to Malegaum having successfully completed his mission. Haji Usman was so pleased with his performance and the skill and maturity with which he had handled affairs that he now promoted him as his General Manager Works. Later that year, an accidental tragedy took place in one of the workers' *mohallas* which provided Haji Usman further proof of Aslam Khan's mettle and leadership qualities.

A Fire Breaks Out

A number of migrant weaver families from Meerut, Awadh and Lucknow had settled down in the Nayapura locality of Malegaum. With successive waves of migration, the area had soon become overcrowded with row upon row of shanties that had sprung up cheek by jowl with each other. These straw and bamboo shacks were little more than one room huts where a whole family lived in dingy and cramped quarters. With increased prosperity, Aslam Khan and his family had moved out of the area to better and more spacious accommodation but Aslam had maintained contact with the worker families who still lived there.

After the monsoon rains, the month of October was hot and dry. It was close to midnight one night and Haji Usman, unable to sleep in the uncomfortably hot weather, was tossing and turning in bed. Suddenly there was a loud pounding noise on the thick wooden door leading to the house from the exterior verandah. Haji Usman jumped out of bed and rushed out to find out the cause for this nightly intrusion.

"Who is there? What brings you here at this late hour?" he called out before opening the door.

"Please sir, come soon," the breathless young man blurted out in between gasps, "a fire has broken out in Nayapura."

Haji Usman went in to alert Sara who was already awake roused by the noise outside. By now the servants were also out and Haji Usman gathered together two men along with the coachman, and accompanied by the young man from Nayapura, they all raced to the site of the mishap where the fire was spreading rapidly through the workers' shacks.

What they saw on arrival was a scene of utter confusion with people running about helter-skelter in all directions. Amidst all the chaos Aslam Khan could be seen with a group of young men that he had rallied around him and organised into a line passing bucket after bucket of water to douse the flames. "Quick, more water over here, over here," the voice of Aslam Khan could be heard above that of the others'. At one point there were loud screams from a burning shack where a woman and her two young children were either trapped or too paralysed by fear to run out and escape from the flames. Without a second thought, Aslam Khan plunged in and came out holding the two children in his arms and rushed in again to lead out their mother.

It appears that the fire had been started by a cooking fire badly extinguished and an item of clothing carelessly thrown over it. The dry heat had been responsible for the quick spreading of the fire. It was soon brought under control and fortunately no lives were lost thanks to the timely action by Aslam Khan and his team of helpers. But the devastation and destruction to the workers' homes and their meagre belongings was total. Not a scrap remained of the homes of twenty-five families and in a matter of a few hours close to a hundred individuals were rendered penniless and homeless.

Haji Usman organized makeshift tents in an open field nearby and the following day with Sara's help, set up a soup kitchen doling out rice and *dal* for lunch and a thick *kanji* broth for the evening meal. This supply of food to the families was to continue until alternative accommodation could be built for the displaced families and they could be resettled in new homes. The land where the shacks had once stood was cleared for fresh construction and Haji Usman hired a *mistri* and masons to start the building work. The rest of the manual work force was hired from unemployed youth from Nayapura and surrounding villages under Aslam Khan's supervision. Within a month five blocks each consisting of five, two room brick and mortar units were ready for occupation. Each displaced family was asked to make a token payment of Re 1 per month to a community chest for the period of one year. This sum represented a small but significant fraction of a weaver's monthly wages and was meant to give him a sense of personal involvement and was also good for his self-esteem.

At the inauguration ceremony of the housing blocks to which some local officials were also invited, Aslam Khan's contribution and his unflinching efforts during the Nayapura fire were recognized and he was presented a purse by Haji Usman amidst rousing applause. In fact, the housing project had been so well received by a grateful weaving community that the following year Haji Usman financed and commissioned 4 more similar housing schemes. The fire at Nayapura had in a sense turned out to be a blessing in disguise.

A Joyful Birth and the
Winds of Change

The month of May 1894 brought unprecedented joy to Haji Usman's household. After a number of heart-breaking miscarriages, Sara gave birth to a beautiful baby girl. Both parents were ecstatic at the arrival of the new born – a pink-cheeked, wide-eyed baby with a dimpled chin. Haji Usman had sent his carriage to Manmad junction to fetch Mariam, his younger, widowed sister who lived in Bombay. She had arrived just in time and had been present at the birth. They named their baby daughter Aisha at a brief naming ceremony on the 7th day after her birth, attended by family members and close friends and presided over by Hafiz Hamza, whose poor unseeing eyes were unable to see the child whose naming he was about to consecrate. Haji Usman guided his right hand as he gently stroked the tiny face and whispered the *kalma of shahada*, or declaration of faith, into the baby's ear along with softly intoning her name into it as well. He then put a small teaspoonful of pure honey into her mouth which she licked only partially before closing her eyes and falling asleep in her mother's lap. After Hafiz Hamza had blessed the new born and blown over her body with the sacred breath of his prayers, sweets were distributed and congratulatory hugs and handshakes were exchanged all around. A goat was sacrificed and the meat distributed amongst the needy. And with that Aisha made her official entry into the world.

Along with Aisha's birth, the winds of change had begun to sweep over Malegaum and by the closing years of the century, the signs of growth and development were to be seen everywhere. In terms of square area Malegaum was the largest *taluk* in the Nasik district and it was soon on the way to becoming the largest weaving centre of the Bombay Presidency. Expansion in the weaving industry was evident from the number of looms which had gone up from 2,441 looms in 1883 to 3,227 looms in 1899 and between the years 1880 to 1890 there had been a 25% increase in the annual volume of local cloth exported out of Malegaum and the figure now stood at Rs. 4,65,000. The population of Malegaum too had risen from 14,402 persons in 1881 to 19,261 in 1891*.

Change was also apparent in the way the weavers had adjusted their techniques and products to changing market requirements. Earlier weavers had only used coarse yarn from the mills in Bombay obtained through local dealers. Now they had access to imported English yarn and went into the manufacture of higher-grade cotton sarees in a variety of hues and with colourful borders. Innovation was also seen in the use of the fly-shuttle loom and the adoption

* The Colonial State and the Handloom Weaver – Douglas E. Haynes

of newer weaving contraptions which enabled more elaborate designs and borders. With these new techniques a number of supplementary industries sprung up for making new kinds of looms and weaving accessories and this added more jobs.

Famine and Plague

B ut the economic benefits of this progress were blunted to some extent by two major catastrophes that hit the region towards the close of the nineteenth century: the Bombay Plague of 1896-97 and the famine of 1899 – 1900.

The famine of 1899-1900 was caused by the failure of the monsoon and deficient rainfall over vast areas of Western and Central India. This resulted in drought, crop failures, scarcities and starvation. Mortality rates were high and countless million individuals died of starvation or accompanying disease. The weavers of Malegaon too suffered extreme distress and famine relief measures either through subsidised grain sales or outright gratuitous relief had to be organized.

For the Bombay Presidency the miseries suffered by the famine were nothing compared to what the region went through during the outbreak, the spread and aftermath of the dreaded plague epidemic. The commercial success of Bombay and its rapid growth led to a large influx of workers. Most of the immigrant workers lived in overcrowded tenements and *chawls* where public sanitation was poor and basic civic amenities lacking. In the maze of twisting by-lanes with open and overflowing gutters, the drainage system was extremely poor and inadequate and various diseases were endemic to these areas. In the dock areas the godowns and warehouses were often filled with rotting grain and rodents and rats had a field day. Rodent diseases were passed on to humans through fleas that lived in the rats and it was suspected that the plague had been imported from Hong Kong where a plague epidemic in 1894 had killed ten thousand people.

The first case in Bombay was detected and correctly diagnosed as bubonic plague in September 1896 by Dr. Acacio Gabriel Viegas. The onset of the disease was characterized by high fever and a painful glandular swelling called a "bubo" in the groin, neck or armpit areas. Death followed rapidly preceded by a drowsy stupor and even delirium. The disease spread rapidly across the city and the death toll was estimated at 1,900 people per week by the end of 1896. The brunt of the plague was borne by mill workers many of whom fled from the city to escape the plague or the rigorous implementation of the measures adopted by the authorities to contain the epidemic. The population of Bombay which was 820,000 in 1891, dropped to 780,000 according to the census of 1901.

The authorities undertook several measures to stop the spread of the plague such as flushing out drains and sewers with large quantities of seawater and carbolic, emptying of shops and grain warehouses and sprinkling disinfectant powder in alleyways and tenements. But some of these measures were extremely severe and caused misery and deprivation to the masses. The campaign for eradication involved destroying several hundred slum dwellings, the segregation and hospitalization of suspected plague cases, evacuation of people, prohibition of fairs and pilgrimages, examination and detention of road and rail travellers and the inspection of ships and their passengers. For the poor workers, the segregation and hospitalization of suspected victims of the plague led to the loss of their jobs or their income. To avoid these measures, victims were smuggled out and their departure ironically led to the spread of the disease.

It was only after the development in 1897 of an anti-plague vaccine in his Bombay laboratory by Waldemar Haffkine, a Russian bacteriologist, that inoculations started being administered and with this, coupled with the other preventive and sanitary measures, the epidemic was finally contained by the end of 1920. But by then it had spread to other parts of the country notably the Konkan Coast, Thane, Kolaba, Poona, Satara, Nasik district (including Malegaum), Ahmednagar and the towns and districts of the Deccan.

Recognition and a Decoration

Haji Usman's widespread welfare projects and charitable work towards the economic and social uplift of the weaving community of Malegaum had not gone unnoticed. On the 21st May 1898, the Viceroy of India, Lord Elgin, conferred upon him the honorific title of "Khan Sahib" in recognition of his services to the citizens of Malegaum. This civil decoration was a great honour and a fitting culmination to over a decade of public service. It was a formal title of respect and honour, and the recipient was entitled to prefix the title to his name. There was a civic reception held in Malegaon in honour of Haji Usman who had become a father figure to many in the community. Little Aisha, now a lively four-year-old, sat proudly on her father's lap amidst the flower garlands and congratulatory speeches. After the felicitation ceremony a large-scale luncheon was hosted by Haji Usman and an enormous *daig* of *biryani* was set up for general distribution.

In September 1898 Haji Usman was invited for a formal ceremony in Bombay at which the Governor of the Bombay Presidency would officially bestow the title on him along with a medal and a citation or *sanad*. Preparations for the journey to Bombay had begun the previous month and on the day of the family's departure large crowds had gathered outside Khan Sahib's home to bid goodbye and happy journey to their beloved patron and benefactor.

They came in large numbers, whole families bringing along with them their women and children. Some bore small gifts of home-made food stuffs and hand-knitted items that the women had learnt to make from Sara and now wanted to give to her as mementos. Some brought their small infants and babes-in-arms to be blessed by Haji Usman and Sara and some bore small hand crafted toys which they presented to little Aisha.

Haji Usman and Sara were deeply touched by this outpouring of love and appreciation from a grateful community. If only they knew that this taking of leave was more in the nature of a final adieu because fate would decree that Khan Sahib Haji Usman and his family were leaving Malegaum never to return again.

The Move to Bombay

In the early part of the 19th century Khan Sahib Haji Usman's father, a wealthy landowner, had moved to Bombay and settled down, like most other early Kutcchi Memon migrants of the time, in the Mandvi and Chakla areas of Bombay. He invested in property in a rapidly expanding community spread across residential localities or *mohallas* which came to be known by the name or place of origin of the settlers, e.g. "Bhujwari Mohalla", "Bhownagri Mohalla", "Nakhuda Mohalla" etc. For his own family's residence, he built a 4-storey building in which he kept the top floor for his own use and rented out the floors below to other families. It was in this 4th floor house that Haji Usman and his sister Mariam were born and where they continued to live after the demise of their parents and until Mariam's marriage and Haji Usman's departure for Malegaum. On the death of her husband and not having any offspring, Haji Usman out of family feeling offered his younger sister the possibility of moving back to their old home. One half of the house was to be for Mariam's occupation and the other half to be retained by Haji Usman for his own use whenever he should be in Bombay. Mariam gladly accepted the offer. Little did Haji Usman realise at the time how misplaced his generosity towards his sister was to be in the context of his own daughter's future.

On their arrival in Bombay in September 1898, Haji Usman and his family settled into the apartments next to Mariam. Having reached the age of four years, it was time that Aisha be initiated into religious practice through a ceremony called a *bismillah* which was to be held on the child reaching four years, four months and four days. Aisha was excited at all the attention she was getting and looked charming, dressed up in bride-like finery in a brocade *kameez* and matching *odhni* lined with a gold wire *zari* border. She had a crescent and star *maang tikka* poised delicately on her forehead and wore gold *jooties* on her feet. Her parents presented her with a gold necklace, gold ear rings and a tiny gold ring and aunt Mariam completed the set with a pair of gold bangles.

This time there was no Hafiz Hamza to do the honours but Mariam had arranged for a *hafiza* for the initiation ceremony and this venerable lady held Aisha's right hand forefinger and pointing at an opened page to the first Quaranic *surah* revealed to Prophet Mohammedan at Mount Hira, prompted her to read the opening words *Iqra* or "Read." There were the usual blessings and prayers read followed by distribution of sweets and the proud parents and aunt were congratulated by all present, who were then treated to a sumptuous lunch.

The following week Haji Usman had his official appointment with the Governor. He looked imposing in his black woollen *sherwani* and gold brocade *Kutcchi pagdi* as he rode up to the Governor House on Malabar Hill. Government House at Malabar Hill was the Governor's official residence since 1883. It was set in an estate of 50 acres at the tip of Malabar Point surrounded on three sides by the sea and consisted of several low bungalows, large lawns and a private beach. The ceremony was a brief one at which he was honoured with the title of Khan Sahib and presented with a medal and a citation, after which he was invited to tea with the Governor.

A Train Journey

The presentation at Government House over and having attended to pending matters in Bombay, Khan Sahib was getting restless and wanted to get back to Malegaum. One November evening of the same year, having finished dinner, he and his wife Sara were sitting enjoying their customary after dinner cup of tea. Aisha had been nursing a bad cough and Sara had already put her to bed.

"Sara, we must make plans to return to Malegaum soon. You know that I have still a lot of unfinished work that I must do" he told Sara in between sips of tea.

"Yes of course, Sait, I understand" Sara replied, "As soon as Aisha's cough is better, we can go back. I am missing Malegaum too and the air in Bombay is not good these days and I fear for Aisha's health"

"Yes, I agree, but here is something I forgot to show you," Haji Usman removed a letter from an inside pocket and passed it on to Sara.

It was an invitation from his cousin Anwar Hashim who two years earlier had purchased a few acres of land in Igatpuri, a hill station situated 2000 ft above sea level.

It was a mere 140 km outside Bombay on the Bombay-Bhusaval railway line and Anwar Hashim's land was situated in the picturesque valley of the river Bhatsa and surrounded by some of the highest peaks of the Sahyadri range in the Western Ghats. Located in such scenic surroundings he had often suggested to Haji Usman that he should invest in some land in the area. He had himself started a fruit farm on his land growing grapes, guava, papaya, figs and different kinds of berries and had set up a unit for making canned fruit and jams. The letter was to invite Khan Sahib to be the chief guest at the opening of his fruit factory and since Anwar Hashim's wife Naseem was friendly with Sara, he had insisted that both of them should be present.

"But... what about Aisha?" asked Sara, concerned. "Her cough is still bad and the weather there will be cold."

"Oh, we will only be away for two days and we can always leave Aisha with Mariam. She's a big girl now and I am sure she won't mind," Haji Usman reassured her. "We can go back to Malegaum on our return from Igatpuri. But please make sure you pack some warm clothes for the both of us. You are right, Igatpuri will be cold."

So, it was decided that they should leave the following Tuesday by the Manmad Express leaving at 8 o'clock in the morning and reaching Igatpuri at 12 noon. Anwar Hashim had said he would send his carriage to meet them at Igatpuri station from where it was a 2 km ride to his farm. Sara always liked to leave a lot of time in hand and so they left for the railway station at Victoria Terminus early in the morning after kissing goodbye to Aisha and leaving her in Mariam's apartment next door.

The first-class compartment was comfortable and they both enjoyed the ride as the train went chugging along and stopping on the way at Thana, Kalyan and Kasara. By the time they reached Kalyan, they were both hungry and Haji Usman bought hot tea and *batata vadas* from a passing vendor. The ride from Kasara to Igatpuri was breathtaking as the train puffed along the Thul Ghat. The slopes of the hills were misty and all around there was lush greenery, flowing streams and a cascading waterfall.

They reached Igatpuri late by 15 minutes but Gaffar was there waiting for them with the carriage and helped them with their luggage. Sara had brought along a silver salver filled with dry fruit and a set of six silver bowls as a gift for their cousins Anwar and Naseem and they left the station happy and looking forward to meeting up with them.

A Fateful Accident

The carriage that Gaffar had sent was in fact a one-horse trap as the road leading to his farm was narrow and steep, with just enough room for the one-way passage of a small cart. On one side of the hill's slope there was a sharp drop to the valley below. Although it was already past noon the air still had a crisp and bracing feel to it, so different from the pestilence filled atmosphere of Bombay.

Sara was dreamily thinking to herself how wonderful it would be if she could convince Haji Usman to invest in some land in this beautiful valley which was after all not so far away from either Bombay or Malegaum, when suddenly there was a shifting of some loose rocks from the hillside which came rolling down in front of their path. The horse startled and bucked and one of the cart's wheels tilted perilously backwards and over the side. Their weight and that of their bags could not allow the cart to hold balance and before Gaffar could shout a warning, the cart careened to one side and went tumbling down several hundred feet to the valley below.

It was late in the evening before they recovered the bodies. Anwar Hashim was in shock and kept blaming himself for the accident. Naseem reminded him that they should immediately send word to Bombay and inform Mariam of the terrible news. At a hurried consultation it was decided that there would be no point in taking the bodies back to Bombay. Instead a local burial according to Islamic rites would be timelier and more appropriate. Thus, it came to pass that Khan Sahib Haji Usman and Sara were laid to rest side by side in the Igatpuri Muslim Cemetery in a simple ceremony without fanfare which closed with the humbling reminder: "We belong to God and to Him we shall return."

The untimely passing away of Khan Sahib Haji Usman and his wife through the tragic and unforeseen accident sent shock waves throughout Malegaum. The news of his death was at first received with shock and utter disbelief and when the truth finally dawned that their beloved leader was no more, there were widespread outpourings of grief in every household of Malegaum's weaving community. A large section amongst those who had benefitted from his charitable works and community welfare projects felt that his burial at Igatpuri had been hastily executed and that his rightful resting place should have been amongst them at Malegaum.

Be that as it may, the grief and mourning at the loss of a man who had worked tirelessly for the progress of his community was unanimous and spontaneous. In the short span of twelve years Haji Usman had achieved significant milestones in the development of Malegaum but, as he had himself once pointed out, much of his work had been left unfinished. To his credit he had put in place the foundations of change and left behind a legacy for a brighter and more progressive future for his people.

On a more personal level the enormity of the tragedy in his premature passing away was experienced by his daughter Aisha, orphaned at the tender age of 4 years and left in the care of her aunt, her father's younger sister, a woman who hardly knew her and had only been present at the time of her birth. How was the future going to unfold for this little orphaned child and how was she going to overcome her great loss? Only time would tell.

PART 3

BOMBAY:
AISHA JAN MOHAMMED –
1898-1934

Gateway of India, Bombay

St. Xavier's College, Bombay

The Two Aishas Meet

Halima was on friendly terms with Mariam, Haji Usman's younger sister, and they would often meet at community functions and gatherings. On hearing the tragic news of the accident and demise of Haji Usman and Sara at Igatpuri in November 1898, Halima felt that a visit of condolence was due on her part. So, one afternoon she went across to Mariam's house and took her niece, Jan Mohammed and Hajra's daughter Aisha, along with her. And it was thus that the two Aisha's met for the very first time in their lives.

Had they not been separated in age by a gap of twenty-two years, they may very well have been like twins so uncanny were the parallels in their two young lives. Born to well-to do Kutcchi Memon parents, both had been named "Aisha", both were orphaned early by the loss of relatively young parents through unforeseen accidents in the course of journeys, both now lived in Bombay away from their original places of birth, and both were being brought up by their respective aunts: - Aisha Jan Mohammed by Halima and Aisha Usman by Mariam.

The older Aisha's heart went out to the grave 4-year-old Aisha and she hugged her warmly. Orphaned as a young sixteen year old herself, she knew exactly what the little child must be going through. She was moved by the pain and the loneliness in those sad young eyes with their deep furrows. How brave and controlled she appeared to be for one so young. She at least had been much older and had been surrounded by two girl cousins close to her own age and the unquestioning devotion and love of her uncle and aunt. The little Aisha had only an elderly, widowed aunt to care for her and someone who was as much a stranger to her as she was to her.

Yet despite all the empathy she felt for the little Aisha, she felt herself incapable and inadequate to meet the situation. She tried to engage the child in conversation and promised to come by again and play with her. But the course of subsequent events in her life and her own failure at reaching out beyond herself and her own preoccupations prevented her from living up to her promise, a regret that re-surfaced again many years later.

Matchmaker, Matchmaker
Find Me a Match

The following week it appeared that Halima's prayers for Aisha were soon to be answered. There was a common saying amongst the community that "marriages were made in heaven, but heaven could not do without the help of Khattiboo." Although said in jest, the fact remained that half the matches amongst the Kutcchi Memons were arranged and made possible through Khattiboo's influence and contacts. For Khattiboo knew anyone and everyone worth knowing in and around the community. She was a large domineering woman with a booming voice and a sharp tongue. She was bold and frank and spoke her mind fearlessly without sparing anyone high or low. All appreciated her matchmaking talents, but few dared cross her or get on her wrong side.

It so happened that one day Halima had an unexpected visit at her home from Khattiboo. After the usual pleasantries were exchanged, Khattiboo shot straight to the point.

"Halima it is high time you thought of getting our dear Aisha married. Do you want her to become an old maid?

She is pretty and sweet-natured. Why have you waited so long?"

"Thank you. You are kind Khattiboo," replied Halima, "but the circumstances so far...."

"Nonsense," Khattiboo cut her short. "I have an excellent match for our Aisha. He is a thirty-year-old man from a good, God fearing family. He has his own cloth business in Chakla Street and is capable of giving his wife and family a comfortable life. What more can you ask for?"

"I will speak to Rehman and see what he has to say. After all he is now as good as Aisha's father."

"Don't wait too long, Halima. Good matches are not easy to find these days was Khattiboo's parting shot as she swept out of Halima's sitting room.

Aisha had been listening quietly to this exchange from a neighbouring room but said nothing to Halima to indicate that she knew the purpose of Khattiboo's sudden visit. That night after dinner and in the privacy of their bedroom Halima told Rehman about Khattiboo's visit and the details of what she had proposed.

"I think it is a very good idea, but we must first discuss the matter with Aisha and see what she has to say," suggested Rehman. He had developed a fondness for Aisha, his late cousin's daughter and felt a certain responsibility for her happiness and well-being. Besides, unlike a lot of his contemporaries, he was broadminded, respected the women of his household and felt that their views needed to be consulted.

The following day both Halima and Rehman were present when the matter was broached before Aisha. She blushed and looked down, lowering her eyes.

"Whatever you think is best. I know that you have my interests in mind and I trust you both totally. After all you are like my own parents."

Halima drew her close and Rehman put his hand over her head in blessing. "I shall find out more about the family and the concerned gentleman before we give our reply to Khattiboo" Rehman said before leaving for work.

The Cherished Wedding Gift

Ibrahim, the young man in question, was the only son of Kutcchi Memon parents who had like many others moved to Bombay from their original base in Bhuj. The spectre of early parental loss had hung over his family as well. With droves of immigrant workers putting a strain on its yet under-developed civic amenities, public health in the colonial Bombay of the 19th century left much to be desired. The incidence of diseases such as cholera and malaria was high and these public health enemies hit without discrimination, the poor as well as the rich, the well-fed as well as the hungry. The average fatality rate of cholera during the last quarter of the 19th century at 1.75 per thousand population was high and both Ibrahim's parents had unfortunately succumbed to the epidemic.

Ibrahim's father had been one of the first Kutcchi Memons of his generation to move out of the community centric *mohallas* on the eastern side of the city. He established his residence in a more cosmopolitan area on the western side, although his business continued to be in the Chakla area close to Masjid Bunder. On his death he had left Ibrahim a prosperous retail outlet in the busy Chakla Street where all the cloth merchants had set up business. Apart from the shop, there was also a pleasant single storey bungalow on Sleater Road, at the time a quiet, leafy street situated just off the Grant Road Railway Station on the Nana Chowk side. Ibrahim's only surviving relatives were his uncle and aunt who lived near the Zakaria Masjid *mohalla*. They were the ones who had initiated the proposal on Ibrahim's behalf using the good offices of Khattiboo.

Rehman had been satisfied with the feedback he had received from his enquiries and he and Halima decided to give Khattiboo the green signal. And so, a few days later Ibrahim's uncle and Rehman along with a few community elders met to formalise the engagement of Ibrahim and Aisha and this was followed by the usual engagement ceremony hosted by the girl's side. Unlike her cousins whose engagement and wedding followed each other in quick succession, Aisha had more time between the two occasions and this allowed the couple the chance to get to know each other.

Ibrahim was a tall man with blunt features and a face that bore a serious, almost stern expression. But behind this apparent hardness was a kind and compassionate nature. The common loss of their parents drew them to each other and Ibrahim's strength and self-confidence seemed to effectively offset Aisha's shy and self-deprecating temperament.

Ibrahim and Aisha's marriage was solemnized in April 1899 with all the traditions and rituals of a typical Kutcchi Memon wedding. Halima and Rehman left no stone unturned to make it a joyful and memorable event for Aisha. A week before the marriage, the bride to be was supposed to be in *mayun* and remain indoors. According to this pre-wedding seclusion, Aisha was not allowed to do any housework and was made free from all errands and chores. She was supposed to stay away from the public view and this period of isolation was meant to help her start beautifying herself for the wedding.

At a ceremony known as the *manjha*, Aisha was dressed in a yellow outfit and *ubtan*, a paste made of turmeric, sandalwood and rose-water was applied to her face, hands and feet. The following day was the *mehendi* ceremony when women from the family and friends gathered around the bride and henna paste in elaborate designs was applied on her hands and feet. Surrounded by so much love and pampering, Aisha's thoughts naturally drifted towards the memory of her parents and a lump rose in her throat as her aunt Halima, lifting her veil partially, put a small sweetened offering into her mouth. As young girls from amongst their entourage sang wedding songs to the accompaniment of a *dhol*, a double-headed drum beat on two sides with the palms of both hands, Aisha also missed her absent cousins Rehana and Rizwana. All the guests were treated to a lunch by the bride's family of *macchi-muthia*- a dish of steamed spiced dumplings made of *bajra* flour in a rich sauce containing a variety of vegetables like egg plant, broad beans, cluster beans, and potatoes and served with fried fish. After lunch the women gathered in an inner room where admiring glances were exchanged at the display of items presented to the bride in the form of clothing, jewellery and other gifts from the bride's family known as her *patcchi* and from the groom's side known as her *pedda*. Prominent in Aisha's *patcchi* was the blue and gold bone china tea service gifted to her by her late parents. Their curiosity aroused, the women gathered around the display and soon the room was abuzz with stories about the origins of the tea service and the tragic maritime tragedy of 1888 in which Aisha had lost both her parents.

The actual marriage or n*ikah* took place the following day when in the morning the representatives of the bride and groom accompanied by two witnesses went to the bride's home to seek her consent to the marriage through a short ceremony called the *Ijab-e-Qubool.* The nikah was performed by a *maulvi* at the mosque where the groom acknowledged his acceptance and the *nikahnama* or marriage contract was signed by both the groom and the bride.

At the evening function, Aisha looked beautiful dressed in her white bridal outfit and gold ornaments with a bright red *bandhni khombi* with intricate *zari* embroidery covering her head. Ibrahim looked handsome in his smartly cut *sherwani* and *churidaar pyjama* with a golden *kutcchi pagdi* on his head. The wedding function ended with the *rukhsati* or leave taking when the bride bade farewell to her family and walked hand in hand with her husband to her new home with the symbolic holding over her head of the Holy Quran for her protection and well-being. It was an emotional moment for Aisha as she tearfully said goodbye to her aunt and uncle, who in the absence of her parents, had been the two most cherished persons in her life. The day after the *nikah* the festivities came to an end with a *walimah* dinner hosted by the groom's family.

A New Home

Aisha moved into her new home with trepidation. She had been pampered with love and care first by her parents and later by her uncle and aunt and apart from the help that she voluntarily offered her aunt Halima, she had not been burdened with any household duties. Would she now be able to take on the responsibility of looking after a house all on her own? How would she get accustomed to her new home and new surroundings?

The house on Sleater Road was a compact though extremely comfortable bungalow with a small garden in front. From the garden steps, instead of an open verandah, you stepped into a covered and enclosed space which served as a long entrée with enough space for two cane armchairs. On each side of this enclosed verandah was a door leading to a small square room on either side which could be used as a study or even a child's bedroom. Beyond each small entrance room were the two main bedrooms with roomy bathrooms. The space in the centre was the sitting room which extended to a dining room. At the far end on one side was a pantry and on the other side a kitchen. The house was well maintained thanks to her late mother-in-law and Amma, an elderly retainer who had been with the family for over 28 years and had known Ibrahim ever since he was a toddler. Aisha loved her new home with its cosy interiors, but compared to Halima's home, the atmosphere around the house was too calm and quiet and needed some life to be breathed into it.

After the passing away of Ibrahim's parents, Amma had had full run of the house and to her credit she had been an excellent housekeeper and had looked after Ibrahim with a possessive tenderness. Fortunately, she was kindly and even-tempered and showed no hesitation in showing and explaining to Aisha details about running the house. Aisha gratefully acknowledged her assistance and relied greatly on her guidance and help on all housekeeping matters. She was lucky also in having an understanding and supportive husband and things soon began falling into place and before long the house settled into a smooth routine.

In the first month of marriage to help the newly-wed bride get accustomed to her new home gradually and not make the separation from her parental home too sudden, it was the custom to allow her to visit her family twice a week and spend the day there. Mondays and Fridays were the chosen two days of the week and Ibrahim would take Aisha along with him in the morning on the way to the shop and drop her off at her aunt's home. Halima would be only too happy to see Aisha for the pangs of separation had been equally hard on her as well. The two of them would spend the day chatting and catching up, and on the appointed day of Aisha's visit, Halima would make sure she prepared one of Aisha's favourite dishes for lunch. In the evening Ibrahim would come to fetch her and they would return home together invariably carrying some home-made item that Halima would have packed for them to take back. Sometimes, Halima would ask Ibrahim to wait for Rehman to return home and then the four of them would sit down together for the evening meal before it was time for the newly-weds to return home.

In the neighbouring house lived a Goan Christian family, a Dr. Francis Lobo and his wife who were of Indo-Portuguese ancestry. The Portuguese had first landed in Goa in the early 16th century and had left behind a marked cultural and religious influence on their overseas territory which they had held for close to 450 years. Mrs. Anita Lobo had been curious to know who her new neighbour was and with Christmas around the corner, she decided it was a good time to make a courtesy call next door. So, armed with an assortment of home-made goodies like Christmas cake, chocolate fudge, *kulkuls* and marzipan she knocked at Aisha's door. And this good neighbourly gesture was the start of a lasting friendship between the two families over the coming years.

The New Century Brings
Glad Tidings

Anita Lobo was a primary school teacher at a convent school and Dr. Francis Lobo had a private practice at a clinic in nearby Grant Road. Anita was good at making confectionary and cakes and Aisha had acquired a certain culinary talent from her mother and over exchanging recipes and cooking demonstrations the two women were soon able to establish a good connect. The following week, came the festival of *Eid* and Aisha decided to reciprocate Anita's gesture by taking along a jug of *sheer khorma* and a plate of *sevian* to Anita's house. This time she asked Ibrahim to accompany her and this provided an opportunity for the two men to get acquainted with each other.

And so, the days went happily by and before they knew it the year was at an end, and with the dawning of the New Year 1900, Aisha and Ibrahim were at the threshold of the 20th century. The start of the new century saw a number of changes in the development of Bombay City. In response to the plague epidemic of 1896, the Bombay City

Improvement Trust had been created on December 9, 1898. Under this scheme a number of measures were undertaken to improve the sanitary and living conditions in the city, to create wider roads, to initiate land reclamation projects and to open up suburbs in the city's north. Alongside these measures, the public transport system was also improved with the introduction of the first electric trams in 1907, the expansion of the suburban train network in 1909 and in 1926 the introduction of motor buses by the "Bombay Electric Supply & Tramways (BEST)" Company.

On a personal front, the new century brought glad tidings for Aisha and Ibrahim in the birth of their first child in June 1901, a chubby 8 lb. baby boy whom they decided to name Isaac. Traditionally the expectant mother would go to her parental home for her confinement. But Aisha explained to Halima that she did not want to leave Ibrahim alone at home and besides Amma was always there. Halima was a bit disappointed, but fully supported Aisha's decision and laughed it off by saying that it would give her more excuses to come check on Aisha in her own home.

Bharda New High School

Aisha's friend and neighbour, Anita Lobo, had also been expecting her first baby at around the same time as Aisha and the two women had spent many pleasant hours together discussing their pregnancies and planning the arrival of their babies. Being a doctor's wife, Anita had many useful tips and her guidance proved invaluable to Aisha. Anita gave birth to a baby boy a week after Isaac's birth and the new baby was christened Roy Gladstone Lobo. Being born within days of each other, they had parallel infant schedules with Dr. Francis Lobo closely monitoring their immunization dates and charts. Living next door, the boys grew up playing together and sharing several common activities and over time a close friendship developed between Isaac and Roy.

Before the parents knew it, it was time to get the boys admitted to school. The choice fell on the Bharda New High School located opposite the Victoria Terminus Railway Station. Established in the year 1891, it was one of the oldest schools in Bombay and certainly amongst the top schools in the Fort area. It had a fine reputation for academics and the overall development of the child. What impressed both Ibrahim and Dr. Lobo was the school's emphasis on discipline and extracurricular activities.

From a young age both Isaac and Roy developed a keen interest in cricket with the Azad Maidan just behind their school providing free and open access for play and practice. By the time they reached senior school both boys were on their school cricket team, Roy developed into a sought-after fast bowler and Isaac into a fine batsman. Interestingly, Bharda New High School in later years was to produce four Indian Test team captains, ample testimony to the school's rich cricketing legacy.

The year 1905 saw the passing away of two individuals whom Aisha had respected and loved dearly and she was deeply saddened at their loss. The first was the faithful Amma whose health had been steadily declining. For the last few years Aisha had insisted that she do no more work around the house, her moral presence as an elder in the home was enough. Amma passed away peacefully at the ripe old age of 74. The other great loss was that of her uncle Rehman who had so steadfastly stepped into her father's shoes. Not only had he been the husband of her aunt Halima, he had also been a first cousin to her late father Jan Mohammed. Rehman had fulfilled his avuncular responsibilities with great understanding and love and he had always stood as a firm rock by Aisha's side through her most difficult times. He was the only man of his generation that Aisha knew who had such a liberal and emancipated view on the status of women. Aisha was going to miss him dearly.

At Rehman's passing away and after the official four and a half month mourning period for his widow was over,

Aisha suggested to her aunt Halima that she come stay with them. Ibrahim was totally supportive of this proposal and Aisha felt it would also be good for Isaac to have his *nani* close at hand. Halima had always had a close bond with her niece who had been brought up as her own daughter and she readily accepted. For Aisha it was in a way a means of repaying Halima for the years of unstinted devotion that she had showered on her.

Birth of a Second Son

Ottone day in April 1907, Isaac now almost six years, came home from school and found that nobody was at home. Not overly bothered he went next door to play at his friend Roy's house, and enquired with Anita Lobo where his mother was. He was told that he was to stay at Roy's house for the next few days as his mother had gone to the hospital but would come back soon with a present for him. Three days later Aisha came back home cradling a new born baby boy in her arms. Isaac was more concerned about his present and asked his mother, "Aunty Anita said that you would come back with a present for me. Can I have my present now, Amma?" Aisha laughed and holding out the baby towards Isaac replied, "Here, this is your present, a new baby brother for you to play with." Isaac gave one look at the infant and turned away disinterestedly. The anti-climax of that first disappointment and its manifest indifference would typify Isaac's attitude towards his younger sibling throughout their growing years and later into adult life as well.

The new baby was named Ismail and his *nani* Halima presented him with a set of gold button studs. His naming ceremony was a small private affair with only close family members present. Ibrahim's uncle and aunt were there, but Aisha's uncle Rehman was greatly missed as was the old retainer Amma. The customary goat was sacrificed for the occasion and the meat distributed amongst the poor and needy. A *biryani* lunch was prepared at home for the family.

One recipient of the *biryani* was a neighbourhood character called Patel who never needed an invitation but somehow always knew the timing of a special occasion or festival when he could call at the house and be assured of a decent meal. One could not quite call him a vagrant or tramp although he did not have a fixed home. He slept in the garage of a large-hearted neighbour whose car he washed each morning and who in addition to a small monthly wage also served him a daily breakfast of tea and a loaf of bread. Apart from that he did odd jobs for the people of the area and relied on the generosity of the neighbourhood homes for the occasional full meal, but there were several days when he had to do without and this showed on his lean frame which bore not an ounce of spare flesh. He was, however, obliging, mild mannered and a harmless soul and was well liked by the people of the neighbourhood, especially the children.

At Aisha's home a mat would be spread out for him in the pantry room and Isaac, and later Ismail, would sit around him whilst he enthralled them with his stories of faraway people and places, never once repeating the same tale twice. The boys would, however, suppress their giggles with difficulty as Patel let out a resounding belch which was meant to show his appreciation of the meal of which he had just partaken.

As Ismail grew up, he proved to be both physically and temperamentally more like his mother Aisha than his father Ibrahim. He had inherited Aisha's fine features and slim body structure and showed more similarity with Aisha's quiet introversion than his father's outgoing gregariousness. This difference in disposition was even more apparent between the two brothers. Whereas Isaac loved sports and the outdoors and could often be boisterous and even overbearing, Ismail was more bookish and loved reading and compared to his older brother he was more reserved, even timid. The six-year age gap and their vastly different natures meant that the brothers had few common interests or activities and were never close.

When Ismail was ready to join school in the 1st standard, Isaac was already in secondary school and was disdainful of his younger sibling whose presence in school he barely acknowledged. They did, however, travel to school together by tram and under Aisha's strict admonishing Isaac would condescend to hold Ismail's hand to help him cross the street.

One day whilst the two boys were returning home from school, Ismail unknowingly left behind his school satchel in the tram. He only realised its absence on reaching home and being greeted at the door by his mother. Isaac was furious at his little brother's apparent carelessness and went off in a huff when he was asked by Aisha to go back to the tram terminus to enquire about the left behind satchel. Having managed to retrieve the bag he came back in an hour and scornfully dumped the satchel at Ismail's feet and threatened, "Next time you do something like this, you will have to go back and get back your bag yourself." Fortunately, that contingency never arose. Hurtful though it had been, Ismail had learnt his lesson well and he never again forgot or lost his personal belongings.

Whilst Isaac enjoyed the companionship of his next-door friend and neighbour Roy, Ismail was never asked to join in their games and found himself increasingly isolated and rejected. His escape and refuge lay in his books and at a young age he turned out to be extremely knowledgeable and well read. He did well at school too and always topped his class especially in his favourite subjects English Literature, Geography and History. Whilst his brother gained laurels on the cricket field, Ismail made his parents equally proud with his academic achievements walking away with several awards at the school's annual prize distribution, including the coveted general knowledge prize. In the year 1919, at the age of 12, he represented his school in the inter-school quiz competition and won first prize.

That same year Isaac cleared his Matriculation Examination and showed a keenness to pursue studies in architecture. Ibrahim and Aisha were supportive and he enrolled himself at the Sir J.J. College of Architecture which had been established in 1913 and was Asia's first architecture school. It was an offshoot of the Sir J.J. School of Art started in 1896. It was a good career choice for Isaac since he showed a natural flair for drawing and draughtsmanship and in 1923 he passed the Government Diploma Examination in Architecture.

The Independence Movement
Gathers Momentum

Whilst the boys were making good progress in their various academic pursuits, the city of Bombay was witnessing a number of events marking India's slow but steady march towards independence from colonialism. In April 1913, a Congress leader Pherozeshah Mehta started "The Bombay Chronicle," a newspaper which played an important role in the national movement. And far across the seas, forty-six-year-old Mohandas Karamchand Gandhi, spurred on by Gopal Krishna Gokhale's insistence that he return from South Africa to dedicate himself to the service of India, set sail for home. On 9th January 1915, accompanied by his wife Kasturba, he stepped off the S.S. Arabia to a tumultuous welcome at Bombay harbour. The city of Bombay, indeed the whole of India, nurtured great hopes that the man who had fought for his fellowmen in South Africa against oppression and racial prejudice through his principles of non-violent agitation, would champion the cause of freeing India from a cruel colonial regime.

The Indian National Congress which had seen its birth in the city of Bombay on the 28th of December 1885, held its annual conference in Bombay in the winter of 1915. Gandhi attended this meeting and stirred all its top leaders with his impassioned oratory. This was the start of a nationwide campaign undertaken through extensive travel throughout the country to motivate and win over every section of Indian society to his cause through his message of peace and non-violence. But the arduous touring of India had exhausted Gandhi and adversely affected his health. In 1919 he was coerced into seeking medical help and persuaded to convalesce at Mani Bhawan, a spacious mansion on Bombay's Laburnum Road, belonging to Pranjivan Mehta, who had earlier supported Gandhi whilst he was a struggling law student in London.

Meanwhile the World War had ended but there was widespread unrest throughout India on the disastrous after effects of the war that had crippled the economy and destabilised the everyday lives of its people. The struggles for independence continued through organised movements as well as spontaneous acts of protest from the common people. The British government fearing violence and attacks from Indian activists, passed a draconian legislation known as the Rowlatt Act which empowered the government with emergency powers through which any Indian accused of encouraging revolutionary activity or dissidence through speeches or writings could be tried in a closed court without a jury and condemned to imprisonment without the right of appeal.

For Gandhi this was an unjust suppression of a fundamental right and he decided to ask people throughout the country to call a one-day strike or *hartal* against the Act. On the 6th of April 1919, Gandhi himself initiated the strike in Bombay, when starting at dawn he led thousands of people to a gathering at Chowpatty Beach. This was followed by mass meetings and processions in other cities throughout India where large crowds marched in silence in a mass movement of peaceful non-cooperation.

Mani Bhawan in Bombay became Mahatma Gandhi's home from 1917 to 1934. Many milestones of India's struggle for Independence were launched from here - the Satyagraha movement, the Swadeshi movement, meetings to launch the Civil Disobedience Movement, as well as Gandhi's fasts for peace.

Aisha's Household is Plunged in Grief

In 1924 the construction of the Gateway of India was completed and on the 4ᵗʰof December this grand gateway located on the waterfront at Apollo Bunder and overlooking the Arabian Sea was officially inaugurated amidst much fanfare. That same day whilst celebrations were in full swing at the Gateway of India, Aisha and Ibrahim's household was plunged in grief. Aisha's beloved aunt Halima passed away that very day after a brief illness. She was 78. Aisha was deeply affected by her aunt's passing away. Her unstinting love and the protective aura of her presence which had enveloped the entire household could never be replicated and it would take the family a long time to get adjusted to her absence.

The iconic Gateway of India which had once represented the "power and majesty" of the British empire and had been used as a ceremonial entrance to India for British viceroys and governors, was ironically in later years to play an emblematic role in marking India's freedom. It was the Gateway of India which witnessed the symbolic exit of the British from India when on February 28, 1948 the last

British serving battalion, the first Somerset Light Infantry, passed through its arches and left for home, marking the end of British rule in India.

But coming back to the present, after its opening in 1924, the Gateway of India became a popular spot for family outings especially on Sundays and holidays. Visitors strolled along the waterfront, walking through the monument's majestic arches and breathing in the fresh salt air of the sea. On the one hand was the splendid view of the harbour dotted with ships and boats of all sizes and on the other hand the stately Taj Mahal Hotel built by Jamsetji Tata in 1903.

It was also from one of the jetties at the Gateway of India that boats departed with passengers bound for the Elephanta Island, about an hour's ferry ride from Apollo Bunder. It was in 1925, in his last year at school, that Ismail joined a school trip with about twenty classmates to the Elephanta Caves. The group assembled at the Gateway of India at 8.30 am and the boys led by a school master, clambered eagerly into the motor boat leaving at 9 o'clock. The sea was rough but fortunately Ismail was not sea sick and enjoyed the ride with the cold sea spray on his face. From the landing point at Elephanta Island they had to walk for about half a mile on a walkway and steps leading up to the caves cut in rock.

The caves are a collection of cave temples mainly dedicated to the god Shiva. The school master had hired a guide to show them around and to explain the significance of the rock cut stone sculptures depicting various scenes from Hindu Mythology. The most prominent amongst the sculptures was a large 20 ft monolith of the "Trimurti Sadashiva" or three-faced Shiva.

It was meant to be a full day excursion and each boy had been asked to bring along his own picnic lunch. After the guided tour the boys had about two hours of free time to wander around or to engage in games and activities of their choice before it was time to take the return ferry back to the mainland.

A Hallowed Jesuit Institution

That year, Ismail now 18 years old, appeared for and successfully passed the Matriculation Examination. His older brother Isaac, who two years earlier had obtained his diploma in architecture, had joined a British firm of architects. They had been extremely satisfied with his work and had sent him off to London for further training. What were Ismail's plans for his own future? Although the shop in Chakla was doing well, Ibrahim had long sensed that his younger son was not inclined to join him in his cloth retail business and had decided to leave him to follow his own destiny. The path before his older son Isaac had appeared to be clearly cut out for him. But engrossed in his own studies and later in his professional activities he had had neither the time nor the inclination to get involved with his younger brother or to guide and counsel him. Ismail now found himself at an odd crossroads in life, rudderless and a bit confused.

Eventually, in June the following year he enrolled himself for the Bachelor of Arts course at St. Xavier's College, Bombay. St. Xavier's College was founded by

German Jesuits in the year 1869. Built in the Indo-Gothic style of architecture, the college was originally run by German priests but during the First World War, they had been forced to leave and their place was taken by Swiss, English and Spanish Jesuits and later by lay educators as well. Although the college had been started as a liberal arts college, in the 1920's science departments were introduced and in the succeeding years the east-west science wing was completed and inaugurated by the Governor of Bombay on 26 January 1926.

St. Xavier's College was located in the Dhobi Talao area of Bombay, a locality which had derived its name from a lake fed by a number of underground freshwater springs where *dhobis* used to wash the clothes of the British soldiers. By the mid-17th century as the city began to expand the lake had been filled up, but the area continued to be known as Dhobi Talao. Not far from the site of the original lake and within walking distance from St. Xavier's College stood the Kayani Bakery & Co., Bombay's oldest and most well-known Irani Cafe. Founded in 1904 by Khodram Marezaban, a Zoroastrian migrant from Iran, it was vastly popular with the students of St. Xavier's for its cheap and wholesome meals and snacks tinged with the unmistakeable taste of Irani culinary culture. The all-time favourite with the students was a breakfast of *chai* and *bun maska*, and for those with slightly larger appetites it was *chai* and *akuri* on toast.

Being shy and reserved by nature and coming from a fairly sheltered home background, St. Xavier's College proved to be a totally new and challenging experience for Ismail. Compared to the smaller and confined atmosphere of an exclusive boy's school, college was a vast sea of students coming from a heterogeneous mix of cultures and backgrounds and coming from places as far afield as Calcutta, Rangoon, Mangalore and Sindh. He had to make several personal and social adjustments and his first year at college was not the happiest.

It was only during his second year that Ismail was able to slowly find his feet. At school as a third language he had chosen Persian and had learnt the rudiments of the language from an indifferent teacher. He was happy to note that at college there was a department of Persian studies and he gladly signed up for Persian as one of his optional subjects. Under the guidance of a brilliant Persian professor he was introduced to the beauties of Persian literature and particularly of Persian poetry. There was also an English Literature Society which he joined and through which he was able to make some friends and gradually integrate himself into college life.

The following year the Royal Shakespeare Company was touring India with a repertory of three Shakespeare plays. Bombay was the first stop in their two-month itinerary and the English Literature Society at college had arranged for its members to attend the performance of the three plays. One of the prizes that Ismail had won during his last year at school was a book with a selection of some of the best known of Shakespeare's tragedies, comedies and historical plays. This book had been his initiation into Shakespeare and he had managed in the course of several months to read and enjoy all the plays in the anthology. Now he hoped that the three plays being performed were amongst those with which he was already familiar. His luck held out because the three performances were of "Hamlet", "Richard II" and "Twelfth Night" all three plays that he had already read.

A New Beginning

In 1930 Ismail graduated from St. Xavier's in the first class with a Bachelor of Arts Degree in History and English Literature. Both Ibrahim and Aisha were extremely proud of their son's achievement and Ismail received a Jaeger-Le Coultre wristwatch as a congratulatory gift from his parents. Once the euphoria of his graduation had settled down, he was faced with the task of looking out for a suitable job. Not having a clear idea of the field of activity he would like to be engaged in, he was willing to let fate guide him.

He spent many hours scanning the appointments pages of the daily newspapers for possible openings. One day his eye was caught by an advertisement from Thomas Cook & Son seeking applicants for the post of a Tours Executive in their Foreign Tours Department. Not having had any previous exposure to the travel field he was hesitant at first but eventually took the plunge and sent off his application with a roughly put together bio data. To his surprise he was called in for an interview the following fortnight.

From humble beginnings in 1841, Thomas Cook & Son had developed to become the world's best-known name in travel. The company had been the pioneers in the field of conducted tours and all-inclusive travel arrangements, which became known worldwide as the complete holiday "package" (comprising travel, accommodation and food). Thomas Cook had opened its first branch in India, setting up offices in Bombay in 1881. They were now looking to expand their operations in their foreign tours department and were looking to hire enthusiastic young college graduates whom they could train and mould according to their company's policies and procedures.

Ismail looked smart in his well-cut grey trousers and navy-blue jacket and tie but was understandably nervous as he stepped into the Thomas Cook office to be interviewed by a stern looking Englishman. But the gentleman soon put him at his ease and Ismail became more relaxed and confident. His prospective employer was impressed by the neatly turned out and well-spoken young man who had an excellent academic record, was well read and showed a good command over world geography and general knowledge. But Ismail had no means of knowing how he had fared after his interviewer thanked him and politely wished him good day.

The good news arrived through the post the following week. His interview had been successful and Ismail had been selected. He was asked to join duty from the 1st of the following month and report to a Mr. David Sadler, the General Manager Tours. Ismail was ecstatic and looked forward with eager anticipation to this new beginning in his life. Under the guidance of his superior he quickly picked up the fundamentals of his new job. He was conscientious and well organised and his meticulous attention to detail proved to be a great asset in his work.

By the end of his second year he was researching new travel destinations, making out tour itineraries and travel schedules, making and following up on reservations for passengers booked on various tours and maintaining client files and records. He was enjoying his work and getting along well with his fellow colleagues and with each passing year he was entrusted with greater responsibilities and was progressing well in his career with the company.

Bernard Shaw's Visit

The year 1933 began with an event that gained a lot of media attention in Bombay and brought a lot of satisfaction to Ismail personally. George Bernard Shaw, the famous Irish playwright, satirist and social reformer had along with his wife set out on a holiday cruise around the world on the Canadian ocean liner "Empress of Britain." The ship made a brief stopover in Bombay between the 8th and 16th January 1933 which allowed Bernard Shaw, now in his 76th year, only a short visit to India, confined to his regret, to Bombay City alone.

Apart from being a very successful playwright (he had been awarded the Nobel Prize for Literature in 1926) Shaw had through his long and eventful life created quite a stir in the British society of his time. He had been an ardent spokesperson for social justice and an outspoken critic of the British ruling classes, the government and even British royalty. Through his carping humour and satirical wit expressed through his writings and plays he had attempted to set right prevailing social evils such as the rampant class distinctions and the poor living conditions of British workers. He had also been a champion of a classless society and equal rights for both men and women.

Being a literary celebrity and a staunch supporter of India's struggle for freedom, his visit to Bombay naturally created a sensation and he was thronged by writers and journalists. Bernard Shaw was a great admirer of Gandhi and his independence movement. The two had met in London in 1931, but this time a meeting between the two was not possible as Gandhi was imprisoned at the Yeravada Jail near Poona. When asked about Gandhi, Shaw was reported to have said, "He is a charming man, an exceptionally clear-headed man.... He is the sort of man who is born, perhaps, once in several centuries, a very marvellous personality."

For Ismail, the visit of Bernard Shaw created in him the eager excitement of an enthusiastic fan. Throughout his college years he had been an avid theatre buff and had never missed an opportunity to attend a performance of his favourite plays. Although he had read and enjoyed such of Shaw's theatre classics as "Arms and the Man," "Pygmalion" and "Saint Joan," he had not had the opportunity of seeing any of them as live performances. With the very presence of the playwright himself in their midst he was now not likely to miss the chance of being at close quarters with the great personality. During the course of Shaw's brief stopovers in the city, a gathering of students and other enthusiasts was arranged near the Gateway of India to allow them an interactive session with him. Shaw was greeted warmly and was friendly and chatty, although he was not at all amused by a sign he noticed at the nearby Royal Bombay Yacht Club, which restricted entry to whites alone.

The year 1933 also proved to be an important one for Ismail professionally as it saw his promotion to a more senior position in his company. In October 1931, P & O (the Peninsular & Oriental Steam Navigation Company) had launched its brand-new passenger ship the Strathnaver on the well-travelled sea route from London to Sydney via Marseilles, Suez, Bombay and Colombo. The imposing new ship with three funnels carried a total of 1168 passengers, 498 first class and 670tourist class. P & O had appointed Ismail's firm as one of their official booking agents and Ismail was now promoted to the post of Senior Executive from the 1st of April 1933 and given the additional responsibility of managing all bookings received by the company for P & O liners.

PART 4

BOMBAY:
AISHA USMAN – 1898-1934

A Four-year-old Grapples with Her Loss

Mariam had wanted to shield little Aisha from the harsh reality of her parents' loss and she tried to conceal the truth from her by telling her that her parents' trip out of town had been prolonged and it would be quite a while before they would return. But at just over four years, Aisha was a perceptive child and showed a maturity beyond her tender years. With the number of visitors coming to the house to offer their condolences, she sensed that something was wrong and that her aunt was keeping something from her. From what she had seen and heard around her she worked out for herself her own explanation for their absence and Mariam was taken aback when one day she came up to her and announced solemnly, "I know Puppho that Amma and Bappa have gone up to Allah. Don't worry I will pray for them." And with this she buried her face in her aunt's lap and for the first and last time gave vent to a torrent of heart-rending sobs.

Mariam lacked the same maternal instincts that Halima had. Not that she was cruel or unkind but with Aisha being with her parents in Malegaum, she had seen the child only once before at her birth. She had not had the opportunity to create any real bond with her and the role of foster mother had in a sense been forced upon her. Aisha being a sensitive child absorbed these nuances and from an early age she learnt to internalise her feelings of sorrow and loss.

To be fair to Mariam, with the untimely death of her husband and being childless herself, her own life had been a lonely struggle and the additional burden of having to bring up her brother's child did hang heavily over her. She had the additional responsibility of being Aisha's legal guardian and had to manage her inheritance from her father until she came of age. Given the circumstances she did try her best to be affectionate towards Aisha, look after her needs in terms of food and clothing and distract her with toys and play things. The latter, however, did not seem to interest Aisha greatly and Mariam soon discovered that the only real pleasure that the child derived was when she was given her little sewing basket with its needles and coloured threads. From a young age Aisha was able to produce imaginative and intricate stitching patterns. Was it a talent she had inherited from her mother Sara?

The other thing that made Aisha happy was playing mother to babies and small children. The tenants on the third floor of their building had a six-month-old baby girl and Aisha loved cuddling her, holding her in her lap and cooing sweetly into her ear. Mariam would often send her down to play with the little girl. It helped distract Aisha and gave Mariam a little time to herself.

When Mariam heard that Aisha Jan Mohammed had had a baby boy, she decided to first pay a visit to her friend Halima to offer her congratulations and then took Aisha along with her to see the new born baby. Aisha now seven years old was delighted and the two Aisha's met again for the second time, although this time in happier circumstances.

A Re-marriage is Arranged

The marriage season the following year had been dull and Khattiboo was getting worried. To keep her business going she would have to think of some form of diversification. Merely concentrating on matches between young men and women in the prime marriageable age bracket would not guarantee her a regular and steady income. Just as she was getting desperate, a chance conversation with a friend provided her with the much-needed way out and she wondered why she had not thought of it earlier. The much-needed solution to her problem lay in widow re-marriage. If she were to look around her, she would find that there were several men and women who were leading lonely and unfulfilled lives after the loss of their better halves. The companionship and support of a new partner would provide them comfort in their autumn years.

"What a brilliant plan," her friend congratulated her. "You know that Mariam, Khan Sahib Haji Usman's sister is still young. Why not put your idea to the test through her."

"Yes, but how will I find a matching male partner?" reminded Khattiboo.

"I am sure something will come up sooner or later," her friend said encouragingly.

The solution came up a month later in the persona of Jameel Ahmed, a 45-year-old widower, who had lost his wife a couple of years earlier and like Mariam had no children. He was seeking re-marriage and was enthusiastic when Khattiboo approached him with her proposal. The following day she called on Mariam and took along her friend to bolster her arguments in case Mariam needed persuasion. Mariam confessed that the idea of re-marriage had occurred to her as well but the thought of Aisha, now 9 years old, made her hesitate. Khattiboo dismissed Mariam's doubts by saying that she had mentioned the child to the prospective groom and she assured Mariam that this did not pose any impediment because Jameel Ahmed had said he liked children. Since there were no elders in the family to guide and counsel her, Mariam said that she would have to gauge the suitability of the match herself at a personal meeting. Khattiboo said she could arrange that without any problem.

So, a meeting was fixed for the following week at Khattiboo's friend's place. On the appointed day, Mariam made arrangements for Aisha to spend the afternoon with the downstairs neighbours. She spent more than the usual time on her toilette and dressed with care choosing an outfit that set off her slim figure to the maximum effect. With her heart pounding she arrived at the meeting place to find that Jameel Ahmed was already there.

He looked dapper in his smartly tailored clothes and black slicked back hair (probably dyed Khattiboo thought). He had a neatly trimmed moustache and a cocky air, but his manners were pleasant enough. The two of them exchanged pleasantries and Khattiboo's friend served tea. More polite conversation ensued, the meeting ended and everyone thanked Khattiboo and her friend for a pleasant evening. Later Khattiboo reported that Jameel Ahmed was quite bowled over by Mariam and wanted to take matters forward. Mariam said she saw possibilities but she needed more time to think things over.

In reality, Mariam had been quite taken up by Jameel Ahmed but thinking of her niece Aisha, she was unable to make up her mind. Two months went by in the process. Khattiboo was getting a little impatient at Mariam's dilly dallying and sent her a couple of polite reminders. Finally, not being able to wait any more she landed up one morning at Mariam's house and said she needed a reply from Mariam one way or another as she had no face to show the opposite party who had been following up with her relentlessly.

Aisha was at home that day and after Khattiboo's departure Mariam decided to tentatively bring up the matter with Aisha. A small smile appeared on Aisha's face and shrugging her shoulders she replied matter-of-factly, "It's alright Puppho. If it is going to be good for you, it makes no difference to me." Mariam was a bit taken aback by the child's nonchalance, but also relieved that the issue appeared to be so easily resolved.

A second meeting between the couple was arranged by Khattiboo at which Jameel Ahmed was at his charming best. A month later in May 1904, the couple was married in a private ceremony and Jameel Ahmed moved into Mariam's 4th floor apartment. Aisha Usman was 10 years old.

Charm Works Its Way

Mariam had literally been swept off her feet by Jameel Ahmed. After her initial hesitation she had succumbed to his charm and was flattered by all the attention she was getting from him. Not having the support of any elders, she had not been able to gather any information about his antecedents, and with constant prompting from Khattiboo, she had plunged headlong into the marriage.

Up to now, Aisha had lived with Mariam in her part of the 4th floor house but with the arrival of the new entrant, Haji Usman's apartment had to be opened up and Aisha shifted her living quarters to her father's side of the house, although for her meals she had to come over to her aunt's apartment. Aisha was only too happy with this arrangement as it minimised the contact she would otherwise be forced to have with Mariam's new husband. Jameel Ahmed had tried to be affable and charming towards Aisha as well, but she was distant and cool without being openly hostile. She secretly detested the sight of him but she forced herself to be polite although she cringed every time she was obliged to address him as *puppha*. As for Mariam, she was totally under

Jameel Ahmed's spell and as far as she was concerned, he could do no wrong. In fact, she often chided Aisha for not being friendlier and more forthcoming towards her uncle.

Jameel Ahmed had had a difficult childhood. His father had been a clerk in a dockside warehouse and with his meagre salary had had a tough time bringing up his family with four young mouths to feed. Jameel Ahmed had had very little access to a proper education being forced to leave school early in order to start earning a living. At the age of 18 years he had left home and struck out on his own. Without much education he was unable to get any steady or well-paid job and he moved from odd job to odd job, but in the process learnt the ways of the world and eventually became canny and street smart.

Fortunately for him he was good looking in a rakish kind of way and he soon discovered that he was attractive to women. He worked on his manners and appearance and learnt he could get ahead by developing his charm through flattery and smooth talk. Women found the new Jameel Ahmed irresistible and he used this to his advantage, moving from one relationship to another, bettering his prospects along the way. Finally, he met and married a woman much older than himself. But the marriage did not last and the woman walked out on him. He was not in fact a widower as he had purported.

Jameel Ahmed actually did not respect women, he only used them. Behind the veneer of affability there was a deep-seated male chauvinism and disdain for women whom he felt should always be subservient to the authority of a male figure. His views seemed to echo the societal norms prevalent at the time which believed that the woman's role was to be confined within the house. The desired virtues sought in the model woman are well summarised in the following extract, although it may well have been Jameel Ahmed talking:

"She should be the means of comfort to her husband. She should bring up and train the children. She should make her home an abode of peace and rest for her husband and the male members of the family, and she should be always ready in time of need, to undergo hardships and suffer privations. She should be a bright example of chastity, courtesy and piety and above all she should be a living personification of righteousness, adorned with modesty and bashfulness."*

Even at the turn of the century formal education and a wider view of society were denied to women and their segregation and isolation was nearly always total and complete. Aisha, approaching puberty, had not been initiated into any form of formal education apart from religious education imparted at home through a female Quranic teacher who also tutored her in the Urdu language.

In order to maintain this patriarchal social order, early marriages were encouraged. Although in 1929 an act was passed which asserted that the earliest legal age of marriage should be 14, in 1931 in the Bombay Presidency, 67 out of every 1,000 married females were girls under the age of 10. This figure of course varied from community to community and those communities in which marriage was arranged at a later age usually encouraged the education of girls.

---

* Al Hijab: or, Why Purdah is Necessary/by H.H. Nawab Sultan Jehan Begum, Nawab of Bhopal, 1858-1930. Calcutta: Printed by Thacker, Spink for H.H. the ruler of Bhopal, 1922.

Taking Charge

Within a few years Jameel Ahmed had ensconced himself securely in Mariam's home and had a firm grip on all the affairs of the household. All decision making was done by him and any new proposal or venture, no matter how small, had first to be approved by him. He also now had full control over all financial matters relating to incoming revenues, financial outlays and spending. Not being gainfully employed himself, he took over the management of Mariam's and the minor Aisha's affairs completely.

Mariam was only too happy to be relieved of this burden and she trusted Jameel Ahmed implicitly and totally relied on his judgment. One evening he brought home some documents for Mariam to sign and she without questioning him put her signature on all the places indicated by him. This hasty and senseless act on her part was to spell doom in her and Aisha's life in the years ahead. Jameel Ahmed hurriedly put away the papers and announced to Mariam that he was hungry and that she should go about serving dinner.

As Aisha turned thirteen Jameel Ahmed raised the question of her marriage. It was the right time, he reasoned with Mariam, to find a suitable match for her and see her settled into her own home where she could serve her husband and raise her children. Mariam did not require much persuasion and she agreed that Aisha was ready to begin life as a married woman. Secretly she felt relieved that getting Aisha married would absolve her of all responsibility of having to look after her.

This time the need to consult Khattiboo did not arise. The third-floor family, at whose home Aisha had spent many happy hours during her early childhood, were extremely fond of her. They came up with a proposal from a family they knew who was looking out for a bride for their twenty-three-year-old son Abdul Rahim. Although the age gap was large, Abdul Rahim was a quiet and scholarly young man who had a decent job working as a lawyer's assistant and they felt he would make a good husband for Aisha. Not surprisingly Aisha was not consulted but merely informed about these plans for her future.

Jameel Ahmed and Mariam seemed for some reason to be in a hurry and after the formal endorsement of the betrothal, poor Aisha was deprived of the joy of an engagement ceremony and the accompanying celebration at her parental home. With Jameel Ahmed holding the purse strings, arrangements for Aisha's wedding were also far from elaborate. She and Abdul Rahim were married in February 1907 through a simple *nikkah* followed by an evening function with only a handful of guests.

Mariam to her regret had not been permitted to include her friend Halima in the list of invitees. The ties of friendship between the two ladies had been maintained through courtesy visits on two earlier occasions which had made it possible for the two Aishas to meet. It would have been appropriate at this time to have Halima and the older Aisha attend the younger Aisha's wedding. But the event passed without Halima or Aisha Jan Mohammed being even aware that Aisha Usman had been married. Would the two Aishas have the chance to meet again? Would it take a gap of almost half a lifetime before they met again?

A Thirteen-year-old Bride

And so, it was that the child bride Aisha moved into her new home, a modest two-bedroom apartment where Abdul Rahim lived with Fathima, his widowed mother. Having been given a frugal wedding, she at least could hold her head high before her mother-in-law as she showed her the carved wooden box of her mother's jewellery and her mother's rich wedding wardrobe that she had inherited, and which thankfully Mariam had prevailed over Jameel Ahmed to let her take along with her to her married home.

Her mother-in-law was a gentle and kindly woman who had been moved when she had heard about the circumstances under which Aisha had been orphaned at such an early age. Fathima was sympathetic and understanding towards her and within a few days the two women got adjusted well to each other. Aisha did not know what she would have done without the support of this good woman, because it was an uphill task as far as her husband was concerned.

Abdul Rahim was a diligent worker and regular in performing his duties at his office. But at home he was quiet and withdrawn, a man of few words who was often lost in his own world and did not like being bothered with the nitty-gritty of home management. With Aisha he was distant and aloof and even in the most intimate moments he was brusque and unsentimental. Not that he was cruel or violent in any way, but Aisha found his indifference hurtful and disturbing and hoped that things would change over time. In the meanwhile, she busied herself with her household duties which fortunately were shared equally by her mother-in-law.

Aisha had no intellectual accomplishments to boast of, but she had a practical, hands-on attitude to life. She showed great maturity and forbearance for one so young. Not allowing herself to delve too long on sorrow or disappointment, she felt that life had to go on and one had to make the most of what one was dealt out by fate. Abdul Rahim loved reading and a typical night after the evening meal was over, would find him absorbed in one corner with his books and Aisha with her sewing kit in another corner with hardly a word passing between them, whilst Fathima snored peacefully in the other room.

Life carried on more or less in the same pattern until an outrageous incident three years later shocked and scandalised the entire neighbourhood.

The Con Man Flies the Coop

Abdul Rahim had left for work as usual and Aisha and her mother-in-law had got busy with their house work, when a distressed and out of breath Mariam appeared in the doorway shaking all over and waving a piece of paper in her hand.

"Just look at this," she wailed thrusting the piece of paper towards Aisha.

Aisha and Fathima tried to calm her down but by now she was weeping hysterically. "What did I do to deserve this?" she sobbed through her tears.

Aisha read the brief and terse message from Jameel Ahmed written in an almost undecipherable Urdu. "I am going away and don't intend coming back" the note read, "Don't bother to trace or find me. It will be best for all concerned."

Aisha couldn't believe her eyes at what she had just read. She fetched Mariam a glass of water and after gulping down a few sips she finally settled down. According to her, she had had a restless night and slept late. On waking up she realised that Jameel Ahmed was not in the house. She called out to him but there was no response. She looked all over and even unlocked and looked into Aisha's apartment but he was nowhere to be seen. She returned to her own part of the house and on entering the sitting room she spotted the piece of paper lying under an ashtray on the centre table.

She froze in disbelief. Now her shock gave rise to panic and fear gripped her insides. She went all over the house once again like a mad woman and looked everywhere, opening cupboards and drawers. All Jameel Ahmed's clothes and personal belongings were missing as well as all the cash and jewellery that was kept in Mariam's inner cupboard drawer. With a cry of anguish, she sank into her bed as the truth dawned on her. Jameel Ahmed had left her and robbed her in the process. But this was only the tip of the iceberg. The worst was yet to come.

Loss of An Inheritance

The incident left Mariam a distraught and shattered woman. The weeks of gossip and whispered innuendos following Jameel Ahmed's flight were unbearable. She was unable to sleep at night and became jittery and nervous and given to fits of continuous weeping. She stopped eating and her health deteriorated rapidly until she became so weak she could hardly move around the house. When Aisha came to visit her, she was shocked and upset at seeing her in this state and decided to stay with her for a few days to nurse her. But all Aisha's efforts were in vain, she was unable to rally her.

In the midst of all this, one morning they had a visit from a man who said he was the rent collector from the new owner of the building and he had been sent to collect the arrears of rent that had not been paid for the last three months. Aisha's jaw dropped in disbelief. What new building owner and what arrears of rent was he talking about? The building belonged to her father. Surely there must be some mistake. She somehow managed to dismiss the man, did not mention a word to her aunt and decided to discuss the matter with Abdul Rahim later in the evening.

The investigations that Abdul Rahim undertook with the help of his office colleagues were to no avail. It was a clear case of embezzlement and misappropriation. On the death of Khan Sahib Haji Usman, all his properties and assets were inherited by his daughter Aisha. Aisha being as yet a minor, her aunt Mariam had been appointed her legal guardian and all the property documents pertaining to his home in Malegaum, his rented properties there and his house in Bombay had been left in Mariam's care. That naive and gullible woman had allowed herself to be hoodwinked and cheated and, in the process, had forsaken her own life and the fortune of her ward as well. Khan Sahib's properties had been transferred from the name of the original owner and sold over a period of time to various new parties and the culprit behind this contemptible crime was untraceable.

But was Mariam the only person to carry the full blame? Was Abdul Rahim, an educated and mature adult not also guilty of negligence and indifference? Lost in his own dreamy world he had never shown any interest in his minor wife's affairs. And poor Aisha, lost between a foolish aunt and an uncaring husband, had been deprived and robbed of her rightful inheritance. As for Mariam, this latest blow was too much for her frail state of health. She passed away in her sleep only a fortnight later.

Tough Times Ahead

Aisha and Abdul Rahim had to arrange and pay for Mariam's funeral and dispose of her few belongings. They also had to pay off the rent arrears and clear out and empty both portions of the 4th floor apartment in a building of which all the floors should rightfully have been in Aisha's ownership. She refused to part with the few possessions and items of furniture that remained to remind her of her parents, although it meant overcrowding their already small apartment.

Aisha had to summon all her inner strength and resilience to weather this latest misfortune which she did with great courage and her usual forbearance. No tears were shed, no denouncements made concerning her loss. She just gritted her teeth and decided to move ahead and face the world. But their financial difficulties kept mounting on account of the accumulated debts and the unforeseen expenses they had had to face.

Abdul Rahim's salary was not enough to meet their commitments and Aisha had to take up sewing and tailoring jobs from the neighbourhood to make ends meet. But still that was not enough to clear their debts. There was a jobless man with a family to feed living on the ground floor of their building. Aisha entered into a business deal with him which would serve the dual purpose of giving him a means of livelihood and also bring her some returns as well.

China silk was very much in demand at the time but not widely available in the clothing shops. Aisha suggested to her struggling neighbour that he go around from door to door and try and sell the silk by the yard to interested women buyers from well to do families. The idea appealed to the man who was not averse to hard work. It may have been the inborn instincts inherited from her late father that prompted Aisha to extend a helping hand to this needy young man. She sold some of her mother's jewellery and with that she bought several bolts of china silk in different colours and shades. Each day the young man would set out with a heavy bundle on his back and return in the evening and report to Aisha the result of his day's efforts. Somehow, they struggled and managed to pull through, clearing all their debts and keeping their heads above water.

A Birth and a Miraculous
Turning Point

In September 1915 Aisha and Abdul Rahim were blessed with a baby girl who they named Rabia, after Rabia Basri the 8th century Muslim saint and Sufi mystic. Rabia's birth, like that of her mother's, was the fruit of several years of yearning and from the first hour of her birth Aisha knew that she was going to be a very special child. She was a beautiful baby with a bright round face, milk white skin, dark expressive eyes and a head covered with soft, light brown hair.

Apart from the joy it brought, Rabia's arrival into the world ushered a miraculous turning point in the fortunes of her parents. An uncle of Abdul Rahim's on his father's side had passed away recently in Madras. One day a letter arrived from this uncle's lawyers stating that the kind old man had remembered Abdul Rahim in his will and left him a small inheritance which he should travel down to Madras to claim at his earliest convenience. So, Abdul Rahim applied for a few days leave from his office and took the train down to

Madras. Fortunately for him his uncle's assets had already been liquidated and the proceeds were being distributed amongst the various beneficiaries. Abdul Rahim was able to return home with a cheque made out in his name and bearing a fairly substantial sum of money.

This unexpected windfall proved to be an ego booster and a big shot in the arm for Abdul Rahim. Whether it was his enhanced financial status or the birth of his daughter or perhaps both, but Abdul Rahim became a changed man. The aloofness and indifference seemed to have disappeared and he started getting more involved in the affairs of the household. Rabia became the apple of his eye. For a man who was often accused of being cold and unfeeling, he was now openly demonstrative of his love for his child. It seemed as if some tightly wound up knot inside him had been let loose and he began to be more attentive towards Aisha as well.

If Rabia's birth had been instrumental in bringing about the change in Abdul Rahim, all around him were reaping the benefits of his changed personality. More importantly it meant that Rabia was growing up in an atmosphere of harmony, wellbeing, warmth and love. Aisha especially was determined that her daughter should want for nothing and little Rabia was spoilt by an abundance of dolls, toys and new dresses.

Abdul Rahim had his own special way of spoiling his daughter. On his way back from work he would pass a small shop which went by the name of "Jewel Chocolates". It had a vast array of chocolates of different shapes and sizes all attractively wrapped in silver foil of different colours and displayed in neat rows of trays arranged in a glass show case. It became a ritual for him to pick up a small packet of chocolates each week for Rabia, choosing a different colour wrapping each time. Rabia loved the chocolates and eagerly looked forward to a different coloured chocolate wrapping each week. The taste for fine chocolates was to stay with her and was turned to her advantage later in adult life.

Their living quarters were proving to be tight and inadequate. Aisha one day cautiously mentioned to her husband that they should perhaps consider moving to larger and better accommodation. To her surprise Abdul Rahim warmed to the idea and said that he would start making enquiries. The following week he came home telling her that a colleague in his office had suggested a flat for rent in a peaceful residential area not far from his place of work and would she like to go out and see it on the coming Sunday.

Aisha fell in love with the place immediately. It was a spacious three-bedroom apartment in a quiet lane off the recently commissioned Lamington Road, named after Lord Lamington who had been the Governor of Bombay between 1903 and 1907. It had a large balcony in front of the living room and smaller balconies in front of each of the three bedrooms. Compared to their earlier house, this was sheer luxury and Aisha was particularly happy for the fact that she was able to comfortably install the furniture items from her father's home, especially a pair of burma teak wood cupboards with elaborately carved cornices. Proudly displayed on her living room wall was the framed citation from the Viceroy of India conferring on her father Haji Usman the title of Khan Sahib.

An Unusual Birthday Gift

For Rabia's fifth birthday her father gifted her with a talking mynah that Rabia named Amina. Amina had a jet-black plumage with a bright yellow beak and bright orange patches on the side of her head. She was an extremely smart bird and could reproduce many everyday sounds and especially the human voice with astonishing accuracy and clarity. Rabia spent many joyful hours teaching her to mimic her voice and even that of her mother and grandmother, sometimes with hilarious results. Over time she could mimic Aisha calling out to her daughter "Raboo wake up," or "hello," "good morning" etc. Often, she would reproduce the sound of a car horn, a creaking door, a dog's bark and even whistled tunes. Rabia's grandmother was less amused when Amina would call "*Dadi* come eat your lunch."

Their improved financial situation meant that Aisha could now conceive of engaging some house help to assist her with the cooking and housework and also attend to Rabia. Hasina was a young woman of about eighteen years from a poor family living in Kalyan, a town about 50 km outside Bombay. Impelled by poverty, these families were forced to send their young women to work as domestic servants in well-to-do households in Bombay. If they were lucky to find a decent family to work for, it provided them with the basic requirements of food, shelter and clothing in addition to the much-needed monetary support which they could send back to their families from their salaries each month. Orphaned as a young child and having experienced deprivation herself, Aisha was always sympathetic towards the problems of the underprivileged. Being naturally generous and kind hearted she was an exemplary employer. She treated Hasina with compassion and as a working companion rather than as a domestic worker. Hasina on her part was quick to respond to Aisha's affection and kindness and in turn did all the work in the house happily and willingly. She was also devoted to Rabia and proved to be an excellent companion and playmate for her.

But it was time now for Rabia to start school. In 1888, an enlightened Parsi lady named Bachoobai Moos had founded a girls' school in the Grant Road area. She had opened the school in rented premises using her own personal funds. The school was called "Miss Moos School" (later named Girton High School) and had limited space and only 10 pupils to start with. But from humble beginnings, by the year 1910 it had 241 pupils and was among the top 12 girls' schools of Bombay. Fortunately, the school was not far from their home and Abdul Rahim got Rabia admitted there.

As could be expected, Rabia's early days at school were a trial for her and each day began with tears and a refusal to go to school. But Aisha persisted and personally accompanied her and waited outside the classroom. Eventually Rabia settled down to the school environment and especially after she made friends with a little *Khoja* girl called Somaiya Dhunjee who also happened to live nearby her own home. Now the two girls would go to school together with the mothers taking turns alternatively to drop and fetch them. School was only half day and after lunch and a short nap, the two girls would often spend the afternoon playing in each other's homes. For Sumaiya, Amina the mynah was the principal attraction to come play at Rabia's home.

Rabia's first outing without her parents was to attend Sumaiya's 8th birthday party. Dressed in a flouncy pink dress with matching pink ribbons in her hair, Rabia presented a pretty picture. She had been anticipating the event all day and finally when it was time to go, she ran off excitedly grabbing Hasina's palm with one hand and clutching the birthday present for Somaiya in the other. She came home full of the teddy bear shaped birthday cake that Somaiya had cut, the delicious snacks that had been served and all the games the children had played. She made Aisha promise that she would have a similar party for her own birthday next time.

An Outstation Trip

It had been a whole year since Hasina had seen her family in Kalyan and she requested Aisha to give her a few days leave so she could go visit them. Aisha had been thinking for some time of making a pilgrimage to the *durgah* or shrine of Baba Abdur Rehman Malang, a Sufi saint who came to India from the middle east in the 12th century A.D. The *durgah* being located near Kalyan, Aisha, after consulting Abdur Rahim and her mother-in-law, decided that the whole family could go along together and, on the way back Hasina could stop back at her parents' home for a few days.

It actually turned out to be quite an expedition, especially for Rabia's grandmother Fathima. Early one Sunday morning they all set out from Victoria Terminus taking the train to Kalyan. The Haji Malang Durgah, venerated by both Hindus and Muslims alike, stood on a broad plateau on the way up to the seventh century Malanggad Fort, located in the Raigad district. The citadel itself was situated on the summit of the hill at a height of 3,200 feet above sea level. To reach the *durgah*, they had to take two tongas to the base village of Malang Gad located at a distance of

13 km from Kalyan station. They reached the base village by 11 o'clock that morning. From there it was a long trek up a winding path of uneven steps. Abdur Rahim bought stout walking sticks for all of them and arranged for a *doli* to carry his mother who would not be able to take the more than two hour climb up.

Along the way they crossed many monkeys who pestered travellers for food. They had been warned not to carry food packets as the monkeys could sometimes be quite aggressive. And sure enough, ahead of them was a couple who had carried a bag with a picnic lunch. They were attacked by a fierce looking monkey who pounced on them and snatched away the food basket. Rabia, frightened, ran to her mother's side and for the rest of the way up held firmly onto her hand.

The first part of the trek up was the most difficult and they had to take several breaks to catch their breath until they halted for a few minutes at the first *dargah* dedicated to one of Baba Haji Malang's companions who had accompanied him on his mission. Here the little party refreshed themselves with some water and fruit juice before starting out again. On the way they passed the Navdirga Mata Mandir and the Ma Sherawali Temple before they reached the second *durgah* of another follower of Baba Haji Malang. Finally, tired and spent the group reached their final destination, the main *durgah* of Baba Haji Malang.

This was a beautiful structure with a high dome and marble flooring inside as well as on the outer courtyard surrounding the shrine. There were some flower vendors outside from where they bought a *chador* with red roses to make as an offering at the *durgah*. The keeper of the *durgah* pulled out a large ledger in which he noted down their cash donation towards the *durgah's* upkeep. It was evening by the time they had finished paying their respects and seeking the blessings of the Baba. They came out to admire the splendid view of the surrounding countryside below.

There were a couple of shacks at some distance from the main building which could be hired as day shelters or for an overnight stay. Abdul Rahim decided to take a shack for the night as they were all tired and hungry and needed sustenance as well as a good night's rest before they could start on their return trip the following morning. The family reached home late in the evening, exhausted but happy and fulfilled at their two-day excursion. It had been Rabia's first train journey and outstation trip.

The Unexpected Visitor

Apart from the poor, unfortunate Mariam, Aisha had no other living relative. Or so she thought, until one day a remarkable coincidence connected her to a long-lost cousin. Aisha had been just four years old when her parents passed away and did not know any better and Mariam too had not talked about or mentioned any relatives.

One of the clients at the law firm where Abdul Rahim worked was a distinguished looking gentleman who came to consult one of the senior partners, in this case the partner to whom Abdul Rahim was attached as an assistant. This gentleman was Sulaiman Hashim, the son of Khan Sahib Haji Usman's cousin Anwar Hashim. Anwar Hashim had been deceased several years earlier but had left his son the farm in Igatpuri as well as some valuable plots of land in South Bombay. Sulaiman Hashim had a knack for buying and selling real estate and had made a fortune in developing properties and constructing residential and office buildings at Kemp's Corner and in the fashionable Malabar Hill area. He had been impressed by Abdul Rahim's neat handwriting and the organised and efficient manner in which he prepared and put together papers for his client and the two of them got along quite well. One evening Sulaiman Hashim dropped by at the office to collect a file that Abdul Rahim had stayed back to hand over to him. Since it was late and well past the office closing time, Sulaiman Hashim offered to drop Abdul Rahim home in his motor car, a Chevrolet Fleetmaster, that had recently been introduced on the Bombay roads.

Arriving at his home on Lamington Road, Abdul Rahim naturally suggested to Sulaiman Hashim to come up for a cup of tea, which he graciously accepted. Abdul Rahim introduced Sulaiman Hashim to his wife Aisha and she prepared and served them tea. As he sat enjoying his cup of tea, Sulaiman Hashim happened to glance up at the opposite wall and his eyes settled on Khan Sahib's framed citation and he couldn't believe what he saw. Being several years older than Aisha, he had a distinct memory of the unfortunate accident on the way to his father's farm in Igatpuri. In later years his father had often talked of the tragedy that had befallen his cousin Haji Usman and lamented the fact that his cousin's sister Mariam had not responded to his several attempts at keeping in touch. He now sprang up from his chair and with tears in his eyes hugged both Abdul Rahim and Aisha. They were both completely taken aback by this sudden and spontaneous gesture on the part of Sulaiman Hashim, until he sat them both down and wiping his tears, he recounted the story of their connection and the re-union that fate had made possible.

There was no turning back after that. Sulaiman Hashim was a generous, warm-hearted and sentimental family man and he welcomed Aisha into his family fold with open arms treating her like a true younger sister. His wife too was friendly and kind and going forward Aisha became a regular and honoured visitor at Sulaiman Hashim's palatial home on Nepean Sea Road. Sulaiman Hashim had three daughters and although all of them were slightly older in age to Rabia, Aisha would often take Rabia along with her and the two of them would spend an entire day there returning home only in the evening. Apart from the company of her three newly acquired girl friends, the house on Nepean Sea Road held many exciting new attractions for Rabia. There was a wide swing in the lounge and a large aquarium tank with a variety of coloured fish before which Rabia stood in fascinated contemplation. There was a wide balcony, more like an open terrace area, where there was a profusion of potted flowering plants and enough space for games and running around and in one corner of the balcony stood a big, orange coloured cage with a large white cockatoo. Rabia could at least hold her own and proudly declared, "Your cockatoo can't even say one word. You should see how my pet mynah Amina talks."

A New Career Opportunity

For the orphaned Aisha, Mariam's role as a surrogate mother had been largely inadequate, if not openly harmful. But her mother-in-law's affection and understanding, the improved relationship with her husband, the birth of her beautiful daughter and now the open-hearted welcome from Sulaiman Hashim, found Aisha an emotionally complete woman.

But if Aisha was basking in the warmth and love of her new-found family, the friendship and professional respect between the two men had also flourished; until one day Sulaiman Hashim asked Abdul Rahim if he would do him the honour of coming and working for him as the manager of his office at Kemp's Corner. Abdul Rahim was flattered but cautious and decided to talk things over with his wife. Aisha felt that the offer was genuine and altruistic. Sulaiman Hashim had no ulterior motive in offering Abdul Rahim the position and after all it would make a big difference to him both professionally and financially. Abdul Rahim had to admit that Sulaiman Hashim's proposal would not only enhance his work status but also mean a sizeable increase in his monthly emoluments and he decided to accept the offer.

On the first of the following month Abdul Rahim reported for work at his new office. It took him several months getting used to the new work environment, the nature of the work entrusted to him and the hostility of his new colleagues. But Sulaiman Hashim was extremely supportive. His instincts about Abdul Rahim's abilities, his honesty and integrity and his capacity for sustained hard work had not been wrong. In due course he was able to surmount his initial difficulties and was ready to shoulder more responsibilities. By the end of the year Abdul Rahim was able to assume the role of office manager, the post which Sulaiman Hashim had envisioned for him from the start.

Close by to Abdul Rahim's office stood Kemp & Co., the iconic firm of dispensing chemists (which gave the name "Kemp's Corner" to the locality around it). It was an impressive one storey building with a double entrance and stood just off the imposing statue of Sir Jamsetjee Jejeebhoy which separated Hughes Road and Ridge Road. It had several high glass-topped counters and a tall weighing machine with a giant dial. Nearby also was Ebrahim & Sons established in 1928 by Ebrahim Merchant, another Kutcchi entrepreneur. His store stocked imported provisions and bakery items which were popular amongst the residents of the area.

The years rolled by and Abdul Rahim gained the appreciation and respect not only from his own colleagues but also from the various external agencies with which he had dealings with. Sulaiman Hashim trusted him unquestioningly and now made him the keeper of the safe which was installed in his private office. But being a proud man, Abdul Rahim never let it be known to anyone either inside or outside the office of the special familial link he shared with the boss. In fact, Sulaiman Hashim went home every day at one o'clock to have lunch at home. On several occasions he would invite Abdul Rahim to join him, but Abdul Rahim, always wanting to keep his work and his personal life apart, would smile and say, "Some other time, sir." He would then sit down at his desk and eat his own lunch from the box that Aisha had packed for him in the morning.

A Culinary Talent Explored

At Rabia's school, at 16 years of age the girls who wanted to study further were promoted to a year of preparation before they appeared for the secondary school certificate examination. Those who were not inclined to study further were permitted to leave school at the age of 16 years. Both Rabia and her friend Somaiya were not scholastically oriented and their parents opted for them to leave school. Both the girls continued seeing each other and would spend hours together in each other's company at either of their homes. With the passage of time, Somaiya's mother realised that they were whiling away their time without doing or learning anything productive. She proposed a private tutor who would come to each of their houses alternatively and teach the girls a home making course in the comfort of their own homes. Aisha agreed that this was a good idea and an Anglo-Indian lady by the name of Patricia Duarte was hired for the purpose.

Mrs. Duarte was a jolly, round-faced and slightly plump lady of 40 years with rosy cheeks and a benign smile. She wore round horn-rimmed spectacles which added to the roundness of her face and her grey hair was pulled back in a tight chignon held together with several hairpins. She was usually dressed in a pastel coloured dress with flowery prints and her feet were covered in ankle length socks and stout walking shoes. Although kindly in appearance she was a strict disciplinarian and did not put up with untidiness, unclean habits and slipshod work. Both mothers hoped that Mrs. Duarte would be a good influence on their daughters.

She came twice a week, once to Rabia's house and once to Somaiya's house and left them enough homework and exercises to keep them busy during the intervening days. Her home making course included cooking and baking, jam and pickle making, needlework and stitching, cutting and tailoring, knitting and crochet and various household tips on cleanliness and hygiene and often just good common sense. Gardening and pottery were optional subjects for which she charged extra and for which classes were held at her home.

Leaving aside the other subjects which Rabia found rather tedious, she took to the cooking classes like a duck takes to water and enjoyed the cookery lessons the most. She won praise from Mrs. Duarte who complimented her for her talent and told Aisha that her daughter had a natural flair for cooking. Rabia enjoyed every aspect of her cooking course and turned out excellent dishes in all the different types of cuisine both Indian and Continental, although she did not particularly care for Chinese dishes. She made excellent cakes, puddings and desserts too which won her appreciation and praise from both her parents. One item which turned out to be quite a favourite with her father was her translucent guava jelly.

"Did you like the guava jelly I made for you bappa?"

"It was excellent, Raboo. In fact, strawberries have started coming down from Mahableshwar and I will get you some tomorrow. Then you can make me some strawberry jam as well." Rabia glowed with pleasure at the praise heaped on her by her father.

The following year, Sulaiman Hashim's wife Zainab along with some of the other wives from her area organised a charity bazaar. They rented out space at a community hall and set up stalls selling various homemade articles prepared by the ladies – snack items, jams and jellies, pickles and preserves, baby clothes and handmade knitted items. Aisha and Rabia too were asked to participate and Rabia spent days preparing her own speciality foodstuffs to be put up for sale. The event proved to be a great success and the ladies donated the proceeds to a women and children's charity.

For Rabia it provided an opportunity to showcase her talents and one of the ladies from the group suggested, "Why don't you start taking orders for your cakes? Also, you make such good jams and jellies and fruit squashes too. I am sure you will have many ready customers."

So, with a little encouragement Rabia and her friend Somaiya ventured forth into setting up a small home catering business which they called "Cakes & Bakes." The initial clientele came from the immediate circle of their charity bazaar group but as their fame spread through word of mouth, they soon had a regular stream of clients.

Somaiya knew how much Rabia loved chocolates and she suggested that they try their hand at home made chocolates. Soon their business expanded to include chocolates as well which were sold with different coloured wrappings: green for mint chocolates, red for cherry, brown for coffee, purple for almond and white for classic dairy milk. Their chocolate range became so popular that the two of them could no longer handle all the work by themselves. To help them meet the growing demand they had to employ two young girls to help in the manufacturing process and an office boy for the deliveries. What had started off as a small kitchen venture had over time developed into a regular and extremely successful cottage industry.

PART 5

DEOLALI:
THE REUNION – 1934

Rabia's Mother, The Younger of The Two Aishas

Rabia & Ismail, 1934

Winding Up a Business

Ibrahim and Aisha's older son Isaac had been retained by the firm of English architects in London and he had decided to settle down in England. Early in 1934 he wrote to his parents informing them that he had met and fallen in love with an English girl and that they were planning to get married in the coming month. The parents had somehow managed to accept the idea of Isaac making England his home, but his latest letter hit them like a bolt from the blue. Aisha in particular was disturbed by the news and expressed her apprehensions to Ibrahim,

"How can we allow this, Sait? What will everybody say? I had been thinking of finding a nice bride for him from our own community and getting him married on his next trip home."

The raised eyebrows from the community did not appear to bother Ibrahim too much but he agreed with his wife that he too had been hoping for a daughter-in-law much nearer home. Finally, after many long and tortured discussions the couple, disappointed as they were, decided that they would have to come to terms with the changing times and their son's decision. After all it was the question of his personal life, and what right did they have to interfere with how he planned to live it? And so, it was that with a heavy heart, Ibrahim sat down to reply to his son's letter giving him their blessings. Secretly though, both Ibrahim and Aisha, now in their sixties, still hoped for a nice Kutcchi Memon daughter-in-law.

With the older son away and the younger one having decided to chart out his future career on his own, Ibrahim decided that it was time he wound up his menswear clothing business. He was able fortunately to find a ready buyer and managed to close the deal with very favourable terms for himself. Ironically, the decision to wind up his business could not have come at a better time because the following week, Ibrahim came home complaining of tiredness and a shortness of breath. His next-door friend and doctor, Francis Lobo, after doing the relevant tests found that his blood pressure was a bit high, probably the result of fatigue and a build-up of accumulated stress. He prescribed some medication and total rest and recommended at least a month's convalescence at a calm and peaceful hill station away from the hustle and bustle of Bombay city life.

An Ideal Choice for Convalescence

Deolali or Devlali appeared to be the ideal choice, a small hill station in Nasik District situated at a height of 1690 ft above sea level, 17 km outside Nasik City and about 200 km from Bombay. It had been set up as a cantonment town by the British in 1861. It had an Army Staff College and was also an area for Rest and Recreation (R&R) for the British troops after finishing their tour of duty and waiting for ships to take them back home to Britain. There was a common joke doing the rounds at the time that soldiers who suffered a mental breakdown caused by the stresses and strains of military life in British India were sent off to a military psychiatric hospital in Deolali to recover. The name Deolali became synonymous with nervous breakdown, hence in colonial slang the idiom "to go doolally", meant to go bonkers.

Being a military town, it was neat and well maintained and with its proximity to Bombay, its good climate and clean, fresh air Deolali very soon became a popular hill station for rest and convalescence. A number of health sanatoriums were built by philanthropic individuals from Gujarati,

Parsee and Memon communities for the welfare and benefit of their members. Their construction and development was made possible by the availability of cheap and plentiful labour from the nearby villages of Belatgavhan, Nanegaon, Bhagur and Sansari.

One such haven of tranquillity was the Fatma Sanitorium in Deolali Camp, built in 1934 and named after a philanthropic Kutcchi Memon lady by the name of Fatmabai Abdul Rehman Moledina Dhuna. Set in idyllic surroundings in a large plot of land dotted with shady trees and flowering plants, it had two driveways, in the centre of which was a block of six large residential cottages. Each of the large cottages had a wide verandah, a central sitting-cum-dining area and two bedrooms with attached bathrooms, one on each side of the central hall. Behind was an open washing area with a passage leading to a kitchen stocked with an assortment of basic cooking utensils. Beside the kitchen was a WC and stone steps leading to a backyard which in one corner had a small chicken coop with an iron mesh door. Further up the driveway and to the right of the large cottages was an open garden area with children's swings and four smaller single bedroom blocks. There was also an office room on the premises and residential quarters for the manager, a gardener's hut, a small mosque and a sweet water well from which the community drew its supply of drinking water.

Families wishing to stay at the sanatorium for periods of two weeks and upwards needed to make advance bookings with the Trust office in Bombay. Ismail undertook the responsibility of booking his parents for the month of April 1934 in one of the larger cottages and promised to take a two-week holiday from work and join them there. Following Amma's passing away, Aisha had taken on a younger woman to work full time and help with the housework. She now made arrangements so that her house help could accompany them on their outstation stay.

Deolali could be reached by main line trains on the Central Railway boarding from the Victoria Terminus at Bombay. Early on the morning of April 1st, Ismail saw off his parents on the "Kashi Express" which made several stops on the way before arriving at Deolali Station by 12 noon. It was lunch time by the time they were finally installed in cottage No 1 at Fatma Sanatorium. Aisha had taken the precaution of taking along a packed lunch and they now sat down to their first meal in the serene quietude of their convalescent home.

The younger Aisha's mother-in-law Fathima, who had been a pillar of support through the trials of her young married life, was now 70 years of age and had only just recovered from a prolonged attack of bronchitis. The doctor treating her had recommended a period of convalescence at a nearby sanatorium and someone had suggested Deolali with its salubrious climate and peaceful surroundings.

An involuntary shiver ran down Aisha's spine when she heard that Deolali was the next stop on the railway line after Igatpuri. For her, the mere mention of that name conjured up too many unhappy memories. But then her cousin Sulaiman Hashim convinced her that Deolali offered the perfect location for recuperation. It was also the place where his grandson was studying as a border at the famous Barnes School and it would be nice if Abdul Rahim could go pay him a visit to see how he was faring. Abdul Rahim protested that it would mean an absence from work but his boss prevailed over him and insisted that he take a month's holiday which would also provide him with a much-needed rest. So, a booking was made for one of the large cottage blocks at the Fatma Sanatorium and the family of four – Abdul Rahim, Aisha, Rabia and her grandmother arrived in Deolali on the 2nd of April.

The smell of fodder and hay wafted through the air as the train puffed into the quaint little Deolali Railway Station. With a halt of just 3 minutes, Abdul Rahim had to be quick and yet careful not to jostle his elderly mother too much, as he bundled out his family onto the platform. A coolie in a red uniformed shirt and cap helped them with their luggage and led them to 2 waiting tongas just outside the station entrance. With tinkling bells attached to the horses' necks the two tongas rolled along swaying from side to side as the horses surged forward covering the short 2 km distance to their destination.

The main large gate of the sanatorium was permanently shut and the driveway was used more as a promenade which the residents used to stroll along or sit by the green wrought iron benches that were spaced out evenly opposite the entrance steps of each cottage. The smaller gate on the other side was the entrance where tongas were allowed access either to pick-up or drop residents. Their two tongas stopped in front of the rear entrance to cottage no 2. The caretaker who had been expecting them rushed forward to assist them and unlock the premises that had previously been swept and cleaned in anticipation of their arrival.

Settling In

By the afternoon of their day of arrival, Rabia's family was already well settled into their new abode which was going to be their home for the next month. Rabia woke up the next morning to the twittering and chirping sound of birds from the tree outside her bedroom window. She thought sadly of her pet mynah who had entertained her and given her so much pleasure for over a decade, until one morning she had found her lying dead and motionless in her little cage. Putting the thoughts of her pet mynah behind her, she got out of bed realising it was time to get her grandmother her tea and help her mother with breakfast.

Abdul Rahim had stepped out for an early morning walk to explore their immediate surroundings. Next door to their sanatorium was a stately mansion called "Homi Hall" built as a secondary residence by a wealthy Parsee family and on the other side was a long passage leading to a small cottage behind which was a large plot of land converted into a vineyard. Abdul Rahim walked up the pathway to the vineyard. The owner was a friendly and enterprising *Bohri* gentleman and the two of them chatted for a while and Abdul Rahim was invited to come visit the vineyard with his family. The vineyard owner offered him a cup of tea, but Abdul Rahim thanked him and said he would come by again with his family. Further up the road was a military dairy farm from where Abdul Rahim picked up some fresh milk and eggs for breakfast.

After breakfast, father and daughter set out towards the local market to stock up on provisions. In the small cantonment area this was just a kilometre away on foot and the two of them took a short cut through an open field nearby. The market was in fact a large covered shed with three rows of vegetable vendors and behind the market there were two small parallel roads where they passed a line of small shops including a meat and poultry vendor, a couple of grocery shops and a few shops selling a variety of household goods. At the corner was a tonga stand and a bicycle hire shop. The aroma of freshly baked bread led them to a popular bakery owned by a friendly Parsee couple who with a ready smile personally served a line of waiting customers. Laden with their purchases, Abdul Rahim and Rabia decided to hire a tonga to take them back home.

Ibrahim and Aisha next door had been less adventurous and far slower in getting around. They had to seek the help of the mali's wife, a pleasant and obliging young woman from one of the neighbouring villages. She was a striking example of the typical village belle with her smooth complexion and flashing white teeth, her swaying hips and her graceful gait as she walked up to Aisha's cottage with the tinkling sound of her tiny anklet bells and a large pot of water balanced perfectly on her pretty head. She introduced Aisha's maid to the local market and helped her make their initial purchases. Aisha was grateful that her maid was a quick learner and by their third day in Deolali the house was already running smoothly.

A Chance Meeting and a Summing Up

In the evening whilst Ibrahim decided to take a walk in the surrounding area, Aisha, now more relaxed and comfortable, stepped outside her cottage to take in some fresh air. She strolled along the neatly trimmed hedges and well-tended flower beds of the front driveway and presently settled comfortably on the green wrought iron bench opposite her lodging. Looking around her she saw a woman and her young daughter sitting on the open verandah of the next-door cottage. She had the feeling that the woman looked strangely familiar. Had she seen or met her before? Perhaps not. It had been a long, long time back and maybe her eyes were playing tricks on her since her vision was not as sharp as it used to be. She found her inability to trace the woman troubling and yet she was certain that their paths had somehow crossed somewhere in the distant past. She shifted uncomfortably in her seat and peered more closely. The woman's eyes held a certain sadness in them but the set of her jaw suggested character and determination. Wanting to set aside all doubts and remembering how years back her friend Anita Lobo had made the first move to get to know her next door neighbour, she decided that she would offer the same neighbourly courtesy and she walked up the steps to the adjacent house and greeted the two women.

The younger Aisha was pleasantly surprised at her kind gesture, greeted her warmly in return and welcomed her to come inside. The two women introduced themselves to each other and Rabia was struck by the odd coincidence that her mother and the kindly neighbour were both named Aisha. The initial introductions over, Rabia left the two women to chat with each other, whilst she went in to make some tea. Imagine her surprise when she came out holding the tea tray to see her mother and the other lady hugging each other and alternatively laughing and weeping in each other's arms. Through their tears and broken exchanges from the past, Rabia was able to piece together the touching story of the remarkable reunion of the two Aishas.

The wheel of fortune had turned a full circle and fate had decreed that the two Aishas should meet again for the third time in their lives after an incredible gap of 33 years. Much water had flowed under the bridges in the interim years. After the untimely death of her parents in the mysterious maritime tragedy of 1888, Aisha Jan Mohammed had been fortunate in finding the protection and love of a devoted uncle and aunt and later of an understanding and supportive husband coupled with the guiding hand of a faithful and loveable old retainer. Family bonding and devotion had seen her through all the difficulties and trials of her early life. But surrounded by so much love and caring she had undoubtedly been a bit cocooned and spoilt and although well-meaning, her introversion did not allow her to reach out easily to others. She was now approaching old age having had a relatively late marriage and given birth to her first child at the age of 29 years. This first child was now 33 years old, married and living in London.

Her husband Ibrahim, strong and confident as he had been, had always been supportive of his wife and through this he had been able to establish a strong and lasting bond in their marriage. He had also adjusted to changing times and allowed his children the freedom of choice to enable them to work out their own individual destinies.

Their younger son, Ismail, had struggled in his growing years with his reserved nature, an overbearing and apparently uncaring older brother and with doubts about his own future career. But he had overcome his initial shyness, become more confident and used his knowledge and education to carve out a promising career with a market leader in the travel and tourism industry.

The younger Aisha Usman was close on the heels of middle age. Orphaned at the tender age of 4 years, she had been married off at the age of thirteen and lost her inheritance through the folly and naiveté of a love-struck aunt who had been her caretaker and legal guardian. But through extraordinary forbearance and resilience, she had managed to tide over the most difficult period in her young life. She had learnt that life can be full of challenges and unexpected misfortunes, but you have to face these trials head on with courage and determination and not allow yourself to be defeated by them. Having gone through difficult times herself, she was sensitive to the troubles of others and had on several occasions nurtured and supported the less fortunate.

Abdul Rahim, her husband, living in his ivory tower, had been too wound up in himself to be attentive to the needs of those around him, until the birth of his daughter brought about a sea change. He had come to realise that no man is an island and cannot be sufficient unto himself. Remaining inside your own shell can harm not only you, but also those around you. Showing and expressing love can inspire love in others and foster a caring relationship.

Rabia, their beautiful and talented 19-year-old daughter, not being academically oriented had used her culinary talents and with the help of her closest friend had established a successful home catering business. Having turned down proposals of marriage from a line of hopeful suitors, she now appeared ready to entertain the idea of marriage. Was Mr. Right waiting in the wings?

A Joyuful Re-union

The re-uniting of the two Aishas generated much joy on both sides and the sharing of the common parallels in their lives created a strong bond between the two women. The older Aisha made plans for a dinner at her house where the two husbands could meet each other and she could have a chance to observe and get to know the young daughter.

The dinner meeting later that week went off well. Ibrahim and Abdul Rahim got along extremely well together. Being involved in an active work life and not used to long leisure hours they both realised that sooner or later time would hang heavy on their hands. They were therefore happy to have found each other's company which would help pass the time and ward off boredom. Ibrahim mentioned that his son Ismail was due to arrive by the end of the following week and they could maybe organise a few outings together. Abdul Rahim agreed and thought of the visit to the Barnes School that he had promised Sulaiman Hashim.

The older Aisha had been bowled over by the beauty and comeliness of young Rabia, and after the guests had departed, she voiced a thought to her husband that she had been mulling over and over in her mind ever since the day she had met the two ladies next door.

"I think that Rabia would be the perfect wife for our son Ismail and the kind of daughter-in-law that both of us have been hoping for. What do you think, Sait?"

"Yes, I too find her graceful and charming. But let us first talk to our son and see what he thinks," cautioned Ibrahim.

At the mention that Ibrahim and Aisha had another and yet unmarried son, the younger Aisha's curiosity had also been aroused and like her namesake she too had entertained the same train of thought. At breakfast the next morning she discreetly and indirectly brought up the subject. Abdul Rahim looked towards his daughter and smiled. As for Rabia, even if there had been a glimmer of interest, she pretended nonchalance.

Ismail arrived in Deolali at the start of the third week of his parents' stay. Aisha was overjoyed at her son's arrival and proudly introduced him to the younger Aisha and her family at a special high tea that she had arranged in his honour. A few days later it was the latter's turn to return the favour and Ibrahim, Aisha, and Ismail were invited over for dinner next door.

Ismail was charming and gracious and showed a new poise and self-confidence acquired doubtless from his professional success and a wider circle of exposure. He was respectful and deferential towards the elders and especially towards Rabia's elderly grandmother who was flattered by his attention and his attempts to draw her into the conversation.

The Deolali air had obviously suited her and she had very quickly bounced back to health. She had been quietly observing and taking in all those around her and everyone was taken aback when she leaned forward and addressed the little gathering, "I am so happy to meet all of you. I have heard from my grand-daughter the stories of the two Aishas, about how the two first met and how they have met again after so many years. I should not be saying this of my own daughter-in-law, but I knew my Aisha as a young 13-year-old bride, faced with so many challenges, but she was always courageous and strong and managed to see us through the most difficult times."

"Thank you Amma. If it wasn't for you, I don't know how I would have survived," the younger Aisha reached out and put her arms around the 70-year-old matriarch. Looking towards the senior Aisha, she continued, "For me you were like the older sister that I never had. I remember you so well when you came to see us after my parents passed away and later when we visited you when your first son was born. I was seven years old at that time, but we never got the chance to see each other again."

The senior Aisha sighed, "I know, that was very unfortunate. We lost touch completely. Being the older one, I should have made sure to maintain contact with you. I had no idea of all the troubles you went through. If only I had known…."

"Now don't go about blaming yourself, the old lady interrupted her. "All that is finished and gone. We have to be grateful to God for having given us this opportunity to be together." And then as if to change the subject, she continued, "What a fine young son you have, Aisha."

Her endorsement of Ismail put across so succinctly did not require further backing from anyone else. But it was the admiring glances that Ismail shot in the direction of Rabia, that left no doubt in the minds of all those present that he had been totally smitten by her.

The Two Families Interact

Since their arrival in Deolali, the two families had already met a few times and their interaction going forward became relaxed and informal. Plans were made for a visit to the Barnes school and the younger Aisha suggested that whilst the men went off on their visit to the school, the three ladies could go to the weekly farmers' market at Bhagur village. Everyone agreed that this was a good idea. Abdul Rahim said that his elderly mother would stay back and he would make a trip to the local market the following day and arrange for two tongas to take them out on their respective excursions.

As it turned out it was the same two tongas that had ferried them to Fatma Sanitorium on their arrival. The two tongawallahs Hussein and Hari were inseparable and always stood side by side at the tonga stand and preferred to operate in tandem whenever the requirement for hire was for more than one tonga. Their two tongas were outfitted in colourful livery and the two mares, Moti and Hira, were gaily accoutred in ribbons and plumes with a garland of small bells around each horse's neck. In the undercarriage of each tonga was a square of jute cloth held in place with knots attached to the four corners that contained the green gram fodder for the horses. The tongas came up at the appointed time, their arrival being announced by the tinkling of their bells.

The Barnes School was a boarding school established in 1925 by the Bombay Education Society. It was located about 5 km from Deolali Camp and set in pristine natural surroundings in a 265-acre plot surrounded by forest. Its first headmaster had been the Revd. Thomas Evans and it was through his vision and foresight and untiring efforts that the school had expanded its curriculum and facilities over the last decade and acquired its present reputation as a highly respected boarding school. Strangely enough it was the year of their visit to the school that was to be his last year there as he retired in 1934 leaving behind a proud legacy. After his retirement, one of the main buildings in the school was named Evans Hall in his memory.

Abdul Rahim was satisfied that Sulaiman Hashim's grandson was doing well at school and the three men were happy to be taken around and shown the school. The ladies too had enjoyed their visit to the farmers' market at Bhagur and had been able to pick up a stock of fresh vegetables and greens. Rabia had noticed the chicken coop in the backyard of the cottage and had bought a pair of squawking layer hens that she took back bundled in a wicker basket.

One day the *mali* brought in a small basket of guavas which he had picked from the tree next to his hut and presented the small offering to Ismail. Ismail graciously accepted the gesture, thanked the *mali* and asked him if he knew of a place from where he could get freshly plucked fruit straight off the tree. The *mali* explained that there was a fruit orchard and rose garden called "Farzandi Bagh," located on the outskirts of Deolali Camp at a short distance of about 4 km. Ismail felt that this represented a good idea for an outing and he discussed the proposal with his parents. Hussein and Hari's two tongas were ordered again and the two families set out for a visit to the much talked about orchard.

The ride to Farzandi Bagh was bumpy and involved a long wait at a railway level crossing to allow a main line passenger train to go past. But the discomfort of the ride was more than compensated for by the beautiful and aromatic surroundings of the orchard and neighbouring rose garden. Farzandi Bagh was owned by an Irani family and had been passed down to the present owners through successive generations. In fact, as Ismail explained, the word *farzand* was derived from the Persian language and meant "child" or "offspring" and its adjective *farzandi* signified "filial" i.e. relating to or due from a son or daughter, like a "filial obligation" or "a display of filial affection."

The orchard was spread over several acres with groves of various fruit trees bearing guava, *chickoo*, orange, lemon and grapefruit. As one walked through the rows of fruit trees accompanied by a *mali*, the ripened fruit could be plucked and collected in a basket which was later weighed and priced at the small office located near the entrance. The neighbouring rose garden was an enchanting paradise and a treat for the senses with a colourful variety of roses from red, pink and maroon blossoms to white, yellow and orange with some dual colour varieties as well. The tour of the rose garden was conducted by the owner himself as he fondly explained each variety, rolling off exotic sounding names such as Florence, Mercedes, Vivaldi, Melody and Darling pertaining to the different rose species and types.

The trip to Farzandi Bagh had been a delightful and an enjoyable experience for all and the families returned home bearing baskets of fresh fruit and bouquets of freshly cut roses.

When Two Hearts Meet

A few evenings later, whilst Abdul Rahim and Ibrahim stepped out to gather provisions from the market and the two Aishas sat chatting on the bench outside their cottage, Rabia and Ismail went out for a stroll to the nearby Temple Hill on Dhondy Road.

The climb to the top was steep and Ismail held Rabia's hand to help her up. At one point, Rabia's foot slipped on a loose rock and she lost her balance. Ismail grasped her by the waist and the two of them were caught in a tight embrace. Rabia went scarlet as a hot flush of embarrassment coloured her cheeks. But she thanked Ismail and quickly regained her composure. The incident, however, helped dispel any awkwardness that may have existed between them and the two continued their way hand-in-hand to the top of the hill which housed a small well-kept garden and a temple dedicated to the Lord Dattatreya. The summit of the hill offered a beautiful panorama of the golf course below and the distant hills of the Sahyadri range. They sat side-by-side by the edge of the hill and chatted for a long time sharing their various activities and interests, their family details and the events that had taken place in their young lives. Ismail was full of praise for the home catering business that Rabia had set up with her friend and Rabia was impressed by Ismail's worldly knowledge, his facility with the Persian language and the work he did at his travel company. On their way back home, they stopped by at a small eatery to share a snack and enjoy a glass of sugar cane juice.

And so, the days went leisurely by in the calm and serene atmosphere of Deolali Camp. The two families enjoyed the slow pace of life, the fresh clean air, the greenery and the open spaces. Before they knew it, the month was over and it was time to head back home. In British military slang Deolali may have had the dubious reputation of being a loony town where soldiers went "doolally", but for the two Aishas it represented a place of joyful reunion, a merger of two families with a common heritage and the continuation of the legacy bequeathed by their departed parents. In the joining together of two young hearts, it also meant for the two mothers a fulfilment of their hopes and aspirations for the future of their children. The departed grandparents on either side, Jan Mohammed and Hajra, Haji Usman and Sara could only have looked down approvingly and given their blessings to this happy fusion.

After their return to Bombay, Aisha and Ibrahim called on Aisha and Abdul Rahim's home with a proposal asking for Rabia's hand in marriage for their son Ismail. No intermediaries were necessary this time and the carrying across of the proposal was nothing more than a mere formality. On the 30th October 1934, Ismail and Rabia were married with the sun preparing to set on the British Raj and a new dawn about to rise on the horizon of an independent India.

Acknowledgements

First of all I owe a tremendous debt of gratitude to my late parents for having preserved and safeguarded for succeeding generations the two priceless family heirlooms from the 19th century. Much of the material of my story was gleaned through the notes and diaries maintained by my father and the oral transmission of anecdotes and incidents related by my mother and my maternal grandmother.

The beginning of my research was the story of the ship wrecked SS Vaitarna or *Vijli* as she was popularly known. What better starting point than sourcing material from *Darshak Itihas Nidhi*, a Gujarat based foundation for the study and documentation of history, particularly of the region. My author friend Chhaya Goswami provided the name of its Chairman, Hasmukh Shah and a family friend, Pradeep Karhade, through his office contact in Baroda was able to get me his updated address and telephone number. Hasmukh Shah was friendly and enthusiastic when he learnt of my pursuit and went out of his way to get me a copy of "*Vijali Haji Kasamni,*" a painstakingly researched book written in Gujarati by Yunus Chitalwala, a retired assistant director of the Archeological Survey of India. Not just that, he was able to get me the telephone number and put me in touch with the author himself, based in Dhoraji in Gujarat. My sincere thanks to both Hasmukh Shah and Yunus Chitalwala for having provided the fuel to kick start my project.

Of the persons with whom I first shared my book idea were my author friends Indira Chandrasekhar, Manu Bhattathiri and his wife Rasmi and my culinary expert and author aunt Salma Hussain. I am truly grateful to each one of them for their guidance, support and encouragement. In a similar vein, my grateful thanks to two professionals from the world of letters, Priya Doraswamy and Aanchal Malhotra and my widely acclaimed author friend John Zubrzycki for their time and patience in providing me with invaluable advice on enhancing and improving the plot line in my narrative.

Lastly and most importantly, my deep appreciation and grateful thanks to my family - my wife Naila, my daughters Maliha and Marzia and son-in-law Deepak not only for their constant encouragement but also for their unstinting help with sourcing material and photographs, proof reading, editorial inputs, suggestions and changes for improving the subject matter and text. Without their support, my book would never have seen the light of day.

Finally, my sincere thanks to Vandana Valsakumar my publishing consultant and Vishnu Priyadarsan Ranganathan my publishing manager at Notion Press for patiently guiding and advising me through the publishing process.

Glossary

abaya	a simple, loose over-garment, essentially a robe-like dress, worn in parts of the Muslim world
ajrakh	a unique form of block printed shawls and tiles found in Kutcch and Sindh
akuri	a spicy scrambled egg dish eaten in Parsi cuisine
bajra	pearl millet
bandhni	a type of tie-and-dye textile
batata vada	a popular Indian vegetarian fast food in Maharashtra
behen	sister
bhakhri	a round, flat unleavened homemade bread
bhida par eidoo	Parsi dish of eggs on okra
biryani	a mixed rice dish made with Indian spices, meat, vegetables or eggs popular among the Muslims of the Indian subcontinent
bismillah	a ceremony celebrated to mark the start for a child in learning to recite the Quran
Bohri	a sect within the Ismaili branch of Shia Islam
bolani	an engagement ceremony performed at the home of the bride to be

bun maska	a slightly sweet bun studded with raisins and layered with butter
chador	cloth wrapped around the head and upper body; at a shrine a floral offering
chai	tea
chawl	a large building divided into many separate tenements, offering cheap, basic accommodation
chickoo	a fruit with earthy brown flesh and a grainy texture
churidaar	tightly fitting trousers worn in the Indian subcontinent
dadi	paternal grandmother
daig	a large copper utensil or cooking pot used in the preparation of dishes such as biryani and haleem
dal	pulses or lentils
dhobi	washerman
dhokla	a Gujarati snack made with fermented batter derived from rice and split chickpeas
dhol	a double-headed drum beat on two sides with the palms of both hands
doli	a chair carried by at least two porters using wooden rails
doodhpak	a kind of rice pudding made from milk, rice, saffron and nuts
durgah	the tomb or shrine of a Muslim saint
Eid	an important religious holiday celebrated by Muslims
gur papdi	a traditional sweet of jaggery and wheat flour made specially during winters
hafiz	a Muslim who has completely memorised the Quran by heart.
haleem	a stew made with wheat, lentils and meat popular in the Middle East, Central Asia, and the Indian subcontinent

halwa	a milk based dessert set with china grass
hartal	a closure of shops and offices as a protest or a mark of sorrow
ifthaar	the meal eaten by Muslims after sunset to break the fast during Ramadan
Ijab-e-qubool	the most pivotal Muslim wedding ritual in which the bride and groom have to give their consent
Iqra	a Quaranic word which means "read"
jahagirdar	landowner
jooti	a type of footwear common in North India and neighbouring regions traditionally made of leather and with extensive embroidery
julaha	weaver
kadhi	a thick gravy made of chickpea flour and yogurt
kalma of shahada	the testimony of faith in Islam
kameez	a long tunic worn by many people from South Asia
kanji	a type of rice porridge or gruel popular in Asian countries
khajuri	a sweet deep fried pastry that is made as a tea-time snack
khichdi	a dish made with rice, dal, spices and ghee
khitchda	a variation of the dish Haleem, made up of goat meat, beef, lentils and spices, slowly cooked to a thick paste
khoja	a Muslim caste of people in India and Pakistan
khombi	a head covering made in tie and die fabric, used mostly in Kutcchi bridal wear
kulkul	a popular Indian sweet delicacy, often prepared during Christmas
kurta	a long loose shirt worn by men and women in South Asia

lagan nu custard	a Parsee dessert prepared during weddings, made of milk, eggs, butter and nuts
maang tikka	a prime accessory for brides, worn on the forehead
macchi-muthia	a dish of steamed spiced dumplings made of millet flour in a rich vegetable sauce, served with fried fish
maharao	variation of Indian royal title maharaja or 'great king'
mali	gardener
manjha	ceremony in a Muslim wedding in which the bride and bridegroom get smeared with a paste of turmeric and sandalwood in rosewater
maulvi	Muslim religious scholar
mayun	A pre-marriage period of seclusion during which the bride is saved from all household chores and is meant to beautify herself in preparation for her big day.
mehendi	form of body art from India, Pakistan and Arabia in which decorative designs are created using a paste, created from the powdered dry leaves of the henna plant
milaya	a heavy embroidered fabric used by women to cover the head
missar	a silk scarf used as a veil
mistri	A master craftsman or construction mechanic
mohalla	A community area of a town or village
momin	a Muslim or believer
moong dal	a type of legume or pulse
musafirkhana	a hostel or home providing overnight lodging for travellers
muthias	a dish of steamed spiced dumplings made of millet flour in a rich vegetable sauce
nan khatai	a type of shortbread biscuit
nani	maternal grandmother

nikahnama	a written document that two Muslim partners must put their signature on in order to legalise their marriage
odhni	a double layer of cloth worn by women as a head-covering scarf
pagdi	a turban or headdress
pakora	a fried snack from the Indian subcontinent
pakwan	a deep fried crisp bread popular as a breakfast dish
patcchi	part of a Kutcchi bride's trousseau given to her by her parents
patel	a community leader
patra	a spicy, sweet and sour Gujarati snack
patra ni macchi	steamed fish and chutney in banana leaves
pedda	part of a Kutcchi bride's trousseau given to her by her in-laws
phirni	a rice pudding flavoured with cardamom, raisins, saffron and nuts
pir	a Muslim saint or holy man
puppha	uncle
pyjamas	a pair of loose trousers tied by a drawstring
rekla	bullock-cart used widely in city transport in colonial India
roat	sweet flatbread made of wheat flour
rukhsati	the traditional send-off of a bride leaving her parental home after marriage
sait	a respectful form of address for Kutcchi males
sali boti	a Parsi mutton curry served with fried potato sticks.
samosa	a triangular or conical fried snack with a savoury filling
samovar	a metal urn in various sizes used to heat water for bathing and other purposes

sanad	a government deed or citation used in British India to honour prominent citizens
saree	a woman's garment consisting of a length of cotton or silk elaborately draped around the body
seer	a unit of weight or liquid measure previously used in India
sehri	the meal consumed early in the morning by Muslims before fasting
sevian	a sweet vermicelli preparation served during festivals
sheerkhorma	a festival vermicelli pudding prepared by Muslims on the occasion of Eid
sherwani	a long coat-like garment worn by men in the Indian subcontinent
shigram	a type of horse-drawn carriage
shrikhand	an Indian sweet dish made of strained yogurt
surah	the term for a chapter of the Quran
taluk	a sub-division of a district covering several villages
taraweeh	special night prayer recited in congregation during the month of Ramadan
tasbih	a Muslim rosary or prayer beads
thali	a metal plate on which Indian food is served
ubtan	a paste made of turmeric, sandalwood and rose-water
victoria	an elegant horse-drawn carriage
walimah	a marriage banquet served by the groom's side after the wedding ceremony
zari	a fine thread made of gold or silver used decoratively on Indian clothing

Printed in Great Britain
by Amazon

40807768R00125